THE
CHEESE
HANDBOOK

═════

A GUIDE TO THE WORLD'S BEST CHEESES

OVER 250 VARIETIES DESCRIBED,
WITH RECIPES

═════

[formerly titled *Choose Your Cheese*]

T. A. Layton

DOVER PUBLICATIONS, INC.
NEW YORK

Published in Canada by General Publishing Company, Ltd., 30 Lesmill Road, Don Mills, Toronto,
Ontario.
Published in the United Kingdom by Constable
and Company, Ltd., 10 Orange Street, London WC 2.

This Dover edition, first published in 1973, is an
unabridged and corrected republication of the
work originally published in 1957 under the title
Choose Your Cheese. This edition contains additional recipes and a new appendix of cheeses.

International Standard Book Number: 0-486-22955-6
Library of Congress Catalog Card Number: 73-77908

Manufactured in the United States of America
Dover Publications, Inc.
180 Varick Street
New York, N. Y. 10014

Preface to the Dover Edition

THIS book, which first appeared over fifteen years ago under the title *Choose Your Cheese*, is still very much up to date. The publication of this reprint edition, however, has afforded me the opportunity to correct several typographical errors, to add some new cheese recipes and to prepare an appendix of cheeses which have come to my attention since the original publication. These are not necessarily new varieties since, in my opinion, a cheese must stay on the market and be consistently sold over thirty or forty years before it deserves that designation.

The last new conception or creation of a different type of cheese is Bel Paese, which was first marketed in 1921. Since then many "gimmick" cheeses have come and gone. Two recently introduced cheeses deserve special mention. These are Boursin a l'Ail, a little cream cheese with green herbs and a suspicion of garlic, and Crème de Rambol, an almost too rich and overpowering white cheese full of fat, studded with walnuts and flavored with the liqueur Kümmel. Perhaps these will endure sufficiently to become new varieties of cheese.

T. A. LAYTON

London, England
February, 1973

Contents

Part I

CHEESE IN GENERAL

CHAPTER I

Cheese in Literature

THEY say it was invented by accident; a merchant from Arabia put his day's supply of milk into a pouch made of a sheep's stomach, hoisted himself upon his camel and clip-clopped over the desert. The beast's ambling movement, the rennet in the lining of the pouch and the hot sun did the rest. That evening the first drink of whey quenched the nomad's thirst and his hunger was satisfied by the curd—cheese was born.

Records show that it was a food over 5,000 years ago; certainly it was made and eaten in Biblical times. It is first mentioned in the first book of Samuel when Saul goes to do battle with the Philistines. David is told by his father Jesse to take sustenance to his brethren: "And carry these ten cheeses unto the captain of their thousand." Then again in Samuel, David is given food by Shobi and others, "And honey and butter and sheep and cheese of kine for David and for the people that were with him to eat".

In the first quotation it says "these ten cheeses of milk", in both instances the word is qualified in such a way that one wonders whether a cow's milk cheese was considered superior to that of any other or if some other food was also given the name of cheese.

Then Job says, "Thou has poured me out as milk, and curdled me as cheese".

Virgil is always mentioning cheeses. "Yet this night you might have rested here with me on this green leafage. We have ripe apples, mealy chestnuts and a wealth of pressed cheese." Again, "There are little cheeses too, dried in a basket of rushes."

But Virgil's longest reference is in his *Moretum*, a long poem devoted almost entirely to describing how a peasant makes a dish out of herbs, garlic and salt cheese: "Near his hearth a larder hung from the ceiling; gammons and slices of bacon dried and salted were wanting, but old cheeses, their rounded surface pierced midway with rushes, were suspended in baskets of close-woven fennel."

A fair number of references to cheese appear in *The Deipnosophists*, which can loosely be translated The Gastronomes. It is by Athenaeus of Naucratis, a town on the left side of the Nile. It was written around A.D. 200 and its interest today lies mainly in the references which are made to early Greek manners and especially—since the whole fifteen books are the record of conversation at a single banquet—of food and table manners.

Sicily was then the great place for cheese; it came from Tromileii in Achea. In a play called *The Sicilian* Philomer says, "I used to think that Sicily could make just this one speciality, its fine cheese".

There was also a cheese, which Zeus drank, called Opias, curdled with fig juice, probably of cream curd consistency.

Cheese was also used to put over meat before it went into the oven.

> But like a beauteous paunch of gelded pig
> Well boild and white, and basted with rich cheese

says Sopater.

Smoked cheese was eaten, so was green cheese (in colour that is), and a delicious kind of bread was seasoned with aniseed, cheese and oil.

Cheese was used in a remarkable dish called a *Myma* (which may well have resembled a haggis) in which any kind of meat cut up in small pieces, ham, onions, common peeled onions, coriander, raisins, silphium (a Mediterranean plant yielding gum resin much prized by the ancients), vinegar, dried thyme and toasted cheese were all mashed up in blood.

Cheese was especially an end dish; a delicacy belonging to the drinking bout and both Athenaeus and Petronius refer to *epideipnides* or last courses.

Lucius Apuleius (born A.D. 123) in his book *The Golden Ass*, mentions cheese also: ". . . while I did greedily put in my mouth a great morsel of barley fried with cheese, it stuck so fast, being soft and doughy, in the passage of my throat, that I was well nigh choked." He also tells us that Hypata, the principal city of

Thessaly, was *the* place for "fresh cheeses of exceeding good taste and relish", so much so that merchants used to journey there to buy cheese and honey for resale.

Perhaps the most important proof of the importance of cheese —and this as far back as 300 B.C.—can be found in a reference to cooking utensils used in that epoch in a play by Anaxippus who was alive around that time. "Bring a soup ladle, a dozen skewers, a meat hook, mortar, small cheese scraper, skillet . . ."

As for cheese cakes, these were all the rage. The island of Samos was famous for them. Athenaeus even gives recipes: "Take some cheese and pound it, put in a brazen sieve and strain it, then add honey and flour made from spring wheat and heat the whole together into one mass."

The nicest must have been *tuniai*, which were cheese cakes fried in oil on to which was poured honey. Mayris, a playwright of the Old Comedy era 500 B.C. in his *Bacchus* says: "Have you ne'er seen fresh *tuniai* hissing when you pour honey over them ?"

The cheese cake was considered as the most suitable food to eat at a wedding feast. At Argos for example the bride was in the habit of bringing the bridegroom cheese cakes which were roasted and served—with honey—to the bridegroom's friends.

There was also a cheese cake called *glycinas* much in fashion among Cretans, made with sweet wine and olive oil.

DERIVATION OF THE WORD

In Dutch the word is Kaas. In German, Käse. In Irish, Cais. In Welsh, Caws. In Portuguese, Queijo. In Spanish, Queso. And all are from the Latin *Caseus*, which even then also stood for a comic term of endearment.

In English it was Cese or Cyse before A.D. 1100. Then in the twelfth century it was Cease or Coese and in the fifteenth to seventeenth centuries became schese, chease, cheise, chies and ches.

"An cyse an buteran ic do," says Aelfric before A.D. 1000. William Langland in his *Piers Plowman* talks of "A weye of Essex chese" in 1377.

In the Lambet Homilies of 1175 "penni per mon wule tilden

his musetoch he bindeth uppon pa swike chese". "Swike" by the way is treacherous.

By about the fourteenth century different types of cheeses were beginning to be recognised: Piers Plowman talks of "Twa grene cheeses" referring not to the colour, but to their state of unripeness.

In the fifteenth century we have one of the first references to more mature cheeses. John Russell, sometime Usher and Marshal to Humphrey, Duke of Gloucester, wrote his famous *Boke of Nurture* which was published round 1460. It is a *Mrs. Beeton* and a How to Behave at Parties Manual rolled into one and here he avers that "Hard chese . . . wille a stomak kepe . . . open"— a laxative in fact.

Between 1500 and 1600 we have the first really useful references to cheese-making in the English language.

Andrew Boorde, having in 1540 published *The Boke for to lerne a man to be a wyse in buylding of his town,* followed this up two years later with *A Compendious regyment or a dyetary of helth.* He tells us that "There is iiii sorts of chese. Grene chese, softe chese, harde chese and Spermyse. Grene chese is not called grene by reason of the colour, but for the newnes of it, for the whey is not halfe pressed out of it."

Spermyse is the word now obsolete for a kind of cheese which Boorde says "is made with Curdes and the juice of herbes" and very good it sounds too.

Boorde gives us in roundabout way the first reference to the Welshmen's fondness for toasted cheese—in other words the Welsh Rarebit.

Fynde wryten amonge olde jestes how God made St. Peter porter of heven. And that God in his goodness suffred many men to come to the Kyngdome with small deserving. At which tyme, there was in heven a grete company of Welchmen which with their reyrakynge and babelyne trobelyd all the others. Wherefore God says to St. Peter that he was wery of them and he would fayne have them out of heven. To whom St. Peter sayde "Good Lorde I warrant you that shall be shortly done". Wherefore St. Peter went outside of heven gayts and cryd with a loude voice, "Cause Babe! Cause Babe!" that is as moche as to say "Rosty'd chese!" which thynge the Welchmen herying ran out of heven a gretefull. And St. Peter went into Heven and lokkyd the dore! and so aparyd all the Welchmen out!

Andrew Boorde also gives us one of the first recipes for cheese cakes: "Take raw chese and grynde it fayne in mortar with eggs. Put powder thereto of sugar. Colour with safrone and put in cofyns (pie crust cases) and bake it."

Next comes Thomas Tusser, the likeable failure. He was described by Thomas Fuller in his *History of the Worthies of England* (1661) as "successively a musician, schoolmaster, serving-man, husbandman, grazer, poet, more skilful in all than thriving in any vocation. He traded in oxen, sheep, dairies, grain of all kinds to no profit . . . yet hath he laid down excellent rules."

The rules referred to are in Tusser's book *Fieve hundreth pointes of good husbandrie* published in 1573 and the cheese section is in "April's Husbandry" which ends with "A lesson for Dairy-Maid Cisley", in the form of ten faults to avoid when making cheese.

It should not be:

(1) Whitish and dry like Gehazi stricken with leprosy.
(2) Too salt like Lot's wife.
(3) Too full of eyes like Argus.
(4) Leathery like Cobblers' stuff.
(5) Hoven and puffed like Cobblers' stuff.
(6) Spotty or lazar-like.
(7) Full of whey or maudlin.[1]
(8) Too scrawling (old English for crawling) with mites.
(9) Too hairy like Esau.
(10) Nor burnt to the pan.

Tusser put all this into a jingle so that Cisley could remember her work better.

> Leave Lot with her pillar, good Cisley, alone,
> Much saltness in white meat is all for the stone.
>
> If cheese in dairy have Argus's eyes,
> Tell Cisley the fault in her huswifery lies.
>
> Rough Esau was hairy, from top to the foot,
> If cheese so appeareth call Cisley a slut.

[1] i.e. lachrymose. St. Mary Magdalen is often pictured weeping copiously.

Shakespeare has most of his references to cheese in the *Merry Wives of Windsor*.

"You Banbury cheese!" says Bardolph to Slender and this confirms the theory that this cheese was known for its thinness.

"Like a Banbury cheese nothing but paring" is a remark in *Jacks Drum Entertainment* by John Marston in 1600.

Note again the supposed Welshman's fondness for cheese. Says Ford, "I will rather trust a Fleming with my butter, Parson Hugh the Welshman with my cheese, an Irishman with my aqua-vitae or a thief to walk my ambling gelding than my wife with herself."

The rest of Shakespeare's cheese references are:

MERRY WIVES

Evans: I pray you be gone. I will make an end of my dinner. There's pippins and cheese to come.

Nym: Adieu. I love not the humour of bread and cheese, and there's the humour of it.

Falstaff: Tis time I were choked with a piece of toasted cheese.

Falstaff: Heaven defend me from that Welsh fairy, lest he transform me to a piece of cheese.

I HENRY IV

Hotspur: I had rather live with cheese and garlic in a windmill, far
Than feed on cates, and have him talk to me in any summer house in Christendom.

HENRY V

Nym: It will toast cheese, and it will endure cold as another man's sword will; and there's an end.

HENRY VI

Smith: Nay John it will be stinking low, for his breath stinks with eating toasted cheese.

TROILUS AND CRESIDA

Achilles: Art thou come? Why my cheese, my digestion. . . .

Thersites: . . . that stale old mouse-eaten cheese Nestor.

ALL'S WELL

Parolles: Virginity breeds mites much like a cheese; consumes itself to the very paring and so dies with feeding his own stomach.

KING LEAR

Lear: Look look a mouse. Peace peace, this piece of toasted cheese will do it.

Pepys in his diary has an interesting reference to cheese; in his Diary for March 2, 1663:

There also coming into the river two Dutchmen, we sent a couple of men on board and brought three Holland cheeses, cost 4d. a piece, excellent cheeses.

Although the story of the Arabian and his sheep's stomach is tenable, it does conflict with the meaning of the curious old Anglo-Saxon word Cheeselip. The *lip* part (or *lyb, lepe, lypp, lib*) comes from the Gothic word Lubjaleisei which meant witchcraft or poison herb lore. In Old Icelandic *Lyf* meant medicinal herb, in Old English *Lybb* meant poison, while in modern German dialect *Lüpp* means rennet. And so it has been conjectured that originally rennet[1] was some herb juice. Indeed the wild flower *Gulium verum*, because of its property of coagulating milk, has the popular name of Cheese-Rennet as well as Lady's Bedstraw.

By half-way through the seventeenth century, English writers were beginning to make mention of cheeses from the Continent. Thus Thomas Muffet, Doctor in Physick, in his *Health's Improvement* (1655) mentions that Parmesan is excellent and evidently believes that it was this cheese which sustained Zoroaster. "Was not that a great cheese, think you, wherewith Zoroaster lived in the Wilderness twenty years together without any other meat?" Although he may have got pretty tired of it, so far as the keeping powers are concerned the feat is feasible, for Parmesans have been known to keep much longer than this—see Part II.

By 1700 the various English counties were making their own individual cheeses, or more accurately the recipes for making them, or descriptions of them, were coming into print. Wiltshire cheese was in the form of a truckle and was very good.

---

[1] The word comes from an obsolete form of *Run*; in French *renne*. The obsolete, save in dialect, verb *earn* comes from the same root stock and means "to curdle milk for making cheese". Hence earning-grass is another name for butterwort whose botanical name is *Pinguicula vulgaris*.

Suffolk cheese did not have a happy reputation; Suffolk Bang it was dubbed, also Suffolk Thump. In 1794 when other cheese was 5*d.*, Suffolk was 3½*d.*; and Pepys says, "I found my wife vexed at her people for grumbling to eat Suffolk cheese."

Essex cheese was unpopular too; both of these counties have had the following rhyme ascribed to their cheese. It is seventeenth century:

> They that made me were uncivil
> For they made me harder than the devil
> Knives won't cut me fire won't sweat me
> Dogs bark at me but won't eat me.

By the 1760s the cheesemaker was recognised officially, and by then, too, the practice of stamping a cheese was being widely practised. Parson Woodeforde records that a big cheese arrived with the King's Arms embossed on its side. At this time, too, the Ramequin or Ramakin was becoming increasingly popular: "small slices of breadcrumb covered with a farce made of pounded cheese, eggs and other ingredients and baked in a pie dish." We wonder what the "other ingredients" were to which Parson Woodeforde refers, but in any event, we consider this to be one of the few dishes in existence which is near perfect *either* as a hot hors d'œuvres *or* as a savoury.

CHEESE IN VERSE

There is quite surprisingly little of it. So little that what there is is always quoted in the equally surprisingly small number of books on the subject.

The most famous of all is in the French language and is by M. Thomas Braun and translated into English by Jethro Bithell.

ODE TO CHEESE

> God of the country, bless today Thy cheese,
> For which we give Thee thanks on bended knees.
> Let them be fat or light, with onions blent,
> Shallots, brine, pepper, honey; whether scent
> Of sheep or fields is in them, in the yard
> Let them, good Lord, at dawn be beaten hard.

And let their edges take on silvery shades
Under the moist red hands of dairymaids;
And, round and greenish, let them go to town
Weighing the shepherd's folding mantle down;
Whether from Parma or from Jura heights,
Kneaded by august hands of Carmelites,
Stamped with the mitre of a proud abbess,
Flowered with the perfumes of the grass of Bresse,
From hollow Holland, from the Vosges, from Brie,
From Roquefort, Gorgonzola, Italy!
Bless them, good Lord! Bless Stilton's royal fare,
Red Cheshire, and the tearful, cream Gruyère.

The next poem really concerns a legend about the pride of Cheshiremen and their product, for a Spaniard on being reputed to have said that his own land was so fine that things could be produced there twice a year, was told that in Cheshire fruit was ripened twice a day—and a Cheshire Cheese was produced.

A CHESHIRE CHEESE SONG

A Cheshireman sail'd into Spain
To trade for merchandize;
When he arrived from the main,
A Spaniard him espies.
Who said, You English rogue, look here!
What fruits and spices fine
Our land produces twice a year.
Thou hast not such in thine.

The Cheshireman ran to his hold
And fetch'd a Cheshire cheese,
And said, Look here, you dog, behold
We have such fruits as these.
Your fruits are ripe but twice a year,
As you yourself do say,
But such as I present you here
Our land brings twice a day.

The longest poem (shall we say jingle?) comes from America. In 1801 the people of Cheshire, Massachusetts, created a huge cheese to give to their beloved President Jackson. It was to commemorate a political victory; that of the Democrats over the Federalists. On September 8th, 1801, the manufacture was announced in Boston's *Mercury and New England Palladium*, as follows:

THE MAMMOTH CHEESE
An Epico-Lyrico Ballad

From meadows rich, with clover red,
A thousand heifers come;
The tinkling bells the tidings spread,
The milkmaid muffles up her head,
And wakes the village hum.

In shining pans the snowy flood
Through whitened canvas pours;
The dyeing pots of otter good
And rennet tinged with madder blood
Are sought among their stores.

The quivering curd, in panniers stowed,
Is loaded on the jade,
The stumbling beast supports the load,
While trickling whey bedews the road
Along the dusty glade.

As Cairo's slaves, to bondage bred,
The arid deserts roam,
Through trackless sands undaunted tread,
With skins of water on their head
To cheer their masters home,

So here full many a sturdy swain
His precious baggage bore;
Old misers e'en forgot their gain,
And bed-rid cripples, free from pain,
Now took the road before.

The widow, with her dripping mite
Upon her saddle horn,
Rode up in haste to see the sight
And aid a charity so right,
A pauper so forlorn.

The circling throng an opening drew
Upon the verdant grass
To let the vast procession through
To spread their rich repast in view,
And Elder J.L. pass.

Then Elder J. with lifted eyes
In musing posture stood,
Invoked a blessing from the skies
To save from vermin, mites and flies,
And keep the bounty good.

Now mellow strokes the yielding pile
From polished steel receives,
And shining nymphs stand still a while,
Or mix the mass with salt and oil
With sage and savory leaves.

Then sextonlike, the patriot troop,
With naked arms and crown,
Embraced, with hardy hands, the scoop,
And filled the vast expanded hoop,
While beetles smacked it down.

Next girding screws the ponderous beam,
With heft immense, drew down;
The gushing whey from every seam
Flowed through the streets a rapid stream,
And shad come up to town.

Then also from America comes the following poem which was inspired by the four-ton Toronto Fair cheese. Author James McIntype was also an undertaker.

We have thee, mammoth cheese,
Lying quietly at your ease;
Gently fanned by evening breeze
Thy fair form no flies dare seize.

All gaily dressed soon you'll go
To the greatest provincial show,
To be admired by many a beau
In the city of Toronto.

May you not receive a scar as
We have heard that Mr. Harris
Intends to send you off as far as
The great world's show at Paris.

Of the youth beware of these,
From some of them rudely squeeze
And bite your cheeks; then song or glees
We could not sing, oh, Queen of Cheese.

Back to England again. Here is Charles Stuart Calverley, 1831-84

BALLAD

The auld wife sat at her ivied door
(Butter and eggs and a pound of cheese)
A thing she had frequently done before
And her spectacles lay on her apron'd knees.

Lewis Carrol in *The Hunting of the Snark:*

His intimate friends called him "Candle-ends",
His enemies "Toasted Cheese".

Then there is another version of the Cheshire Cheese legend, a long poem by C. H. Longrigg. It ends as follows:

"My land" quoth the Spaniard "bears crops twice a year
Rich produce and fruits and wine that will cheer
The heart of a man. There's no such in thine."
Jack Chester stepped out and soon brought in a fine
Large Cheshire Cheese and said he "Now look you here
Your country produces rich crops twice a year
Of this that I bring in my hands I may say
My country produces rich crops twice a day."

CHEESE IN HISTORY

This sustaining product has only once, to my knowledge, caused a riot and that was in September, 1766, in Leicestershire. This was a time of the year when food was scarce and in this particular year there was real want, and yet Mr. Pridmore, cheese factor of Market Harborough, against the advice of the Magistrate decided to store a large quantity of cheese he had bought, at the Old Bell Inn in the town of Leicester. Storing it was bad enough, but when, a few days before the long established annual fair in Leicester, he decided to move it to Market Harborough, the citizens could no longer be restrained. The first waggon was stopped before it had reached Hunstanton Gate and women distributed the cheese to the crowd. Then the rioters went to the Bell Yard and broke into the warehouse, but by then the Magistrate had arrived and the free issue was stopped.

But the affair later in the day did get more serious; eventually the Riot Act had to be read and Hunstanton Gate cleared, while a whole local regiment was mustered to remove the cheese to the Market-place exchange. None the less by nine that evening, there were 4,000 rioters and next morning four women were put on trial and sent to jail. Eventually order was restored and Mr. Pridmore was allowed to once again cope with his Leicester cheese.

GIANT CHEESES

Mammoth cheeses have long had a fascination for the cheese-maker and, as the poems previously quoted show, America has played her share in producing these huge affairs. In 1801, President Jefferson was presented with a pretty big one on the village green of Cheshire, Massachusetts. Bigger than this was one presented to President Jackson which for weeks stood in state in the hall of the White House. Eventually the floor was six inches deep with fragments chipped by loyal Democrats after they had eaten their fill.

To the fair at Toronto, Canada, some seventy-five years ago, there was sent a cheese weighing four tons, but this was capped by a Cheddar sent to the New York State Fair in 1937.

America has not had it all her own way, for our own Royalty have had monster cheeses presented to them too. In 1825, the Duke of York was given a big Cheshire of 149 pounds, and a little later Queen Victoria, as a wedding gift, was given one weighing over a thousand pounds, made from the entire day's milking of 800 cows. Actually, it created quite a stir and a row, because the donors were so proud of it that they asked the Queen if they could "borrow" it for a while to exhibit. The Queen said Yes, but she went further and refused to take it under her wing when it had finished its publicity round of the Shires of England. The donors thereupon quarrelled among themselves and there was even a court case about it.

A FRENCH WRITER ON CHEESE

Let the last words on the subject be by Emile Zola:

"A giant Cantal, seeming to have been chopped open with an

axe, stood aside of a golden-hued Chester and a Swiss Gruyère resembling the wheel of a Roman chariot. There were Dutch Edams, round and blood-red, and Port-Saluts lined up like soldiers on parade. Three Bries, side by side, suggested phases of the moon; two of them, very dry, were amber-coloured and 'full', and the third, in its second quarter, was runny and creamy, with a 'milky way' which no human barrier seemed able to restrain. And all the while majestic Roqueforts looked down with princely contempt upon the other, through the glass of their crystal covers."

It does indeed seem curious that a food so ancient, so universal, so much liked should have had so little written about it.

CHAPTER II

How Cheese is Made

A VISIT TO CHEDDAR

PILGRIMAGES usually disappoint; you save up in middle age to visit some place which has fired the youthful imagination only to discover squalor, or that you cannot see the shrine for the sightseers.

As for Cheddar, this messy, straggling, dreary little village must be one of the worst examples of an unworthy place giving its name to something which is *hors concours* in its class; for a matured farmhouse Cheddar, made from the flush summer grass milk from Ayrshire or Shorthorn cows, is a marvel. One is apt to describe a place which does not take the fancy as "looking as though a bomb had hit it". Cheddar does not look like that, but after walking down the main street you come to the conclusion that this is its only hope of salvation. At one entrance to the village is a grocer specialising—inevitably—in the product which got its name from the place. The result is deplorable. Single pound and even half-pound "truckles", those monstrous midgets which all true farmhouse cheese-makers despise, straggle on a slimy marble slab cheek by jowl with process cheese, and (when I was there) a weeping slice of Danish Blue.

How the cheese came to be called after the village, not a soul in the place knows, or of course cares. And furthermore, there seems to be little evidence that in the near surrounding countryside fine cheeses have ever been produced.

Most locals don't know that fine farmhouse cheeses are still being made in the country; they think that the highest point of caseous perfection is reached in the "creameries", a horrid name for those huge white impersonal morgues where an effort is made (to be fair, with reasonable success) to produce farmhouse cheese on a massive scale.

Actually legend in this mystery comes slightly to the rescue, for it is said that some milk being left by accident in one of the innumerable caves in the Gorge turned into a superb cheese.

The true home town of Cheddar is Wells, a beautiful bustling cathedral city with a charm surpassed only by Bath itself. Here trades one of the largest suppliers of cheese-making equipment in the country, also one of the very few private cheese factors left in the industry. A few miles away is Shepton Mallet and if you make on a map circles around these towns you will find that they take in the best farmhouse Cheddar-making establishments of the district.

Here in small farmhouses, but under spotlessly clean conditions, exists a craft which because of the urge to mass-produce is one that cannot last much longer, but which, while it lasts, is worth studying.

HOW ALL CHEESE IS MADE

You cannot state categorically how many *main* different types of cheeses there are, any more than you can of insects, flowers or grasses. France has 300 names alone. Many are different names for the same cheese. Others are different shapes for the same type.

But one expert—who had better remain anonymous—has given the following as the main varieties of cheese in the world, stating firmly that "such a grouping is imperfect and incomplete": Camembert, Cheddar, Cottage Cream, Edam, Handkäse, Limburger, Neufchâtel, Parmesan, Provolone, Romano, Roquefort, Sapsago, Gruyère, Trappist.

Basically all cheese is a process of adding a starter, turning the milk into a junket by adding rennet, separating the liquid (whey) from the solid (curd), adding salt and maturing what is left.

Let us take it in more detail in a typical farm ten miles from Wells.

MAKING CHEDDAR CHEESE

The main operation takes place in an outbuilding, usually semi-detached to the house, and about the size of a small billiard room. The room will be whitewashed and will always be clean. Round the walls will be 10, 20, 50 or 100 bright square cards about 9 inches by 6 inches, usually blue, red, white or green and with silver or gold embossed letters to show that the farmer has won a first, second, third, prize at local or big shows of every sort, and that he has had dozens of "recommendeds" besides.

In the centre of the room will be two oblong stainless steel tanks. One very roughly will be 2 yards long, a yard wide and a yard deep. The other will be somewhat smaller. The reason there are two is to be able to switch from the larger to the smaller when the milk yield goes down in the winter and vice versa in the summer. The reason we say "roughly" is that the tanks (vats is the official name) can be supplied in sizes from 50 gallons upwards, while those used by the Milk Marketing Board start at around 1,000 (one thousand gallons). These tanks are jacketed and the turn of a tap brings in steam from pipes from a boiler usually situated in a room adjoining the dairy.

Along one side of the room are the draining boards. These are long flat sinks with iron slabs on them from which more whey drains after the curd has been cut.

Then in an alcove, usually under a window, is some chemical apparatus. A pipette, a big thermometer, a few bottles, a long thin measuring glass. Also there is a record book. Let us look at it; it tells a tale. There are 31 lines ruled across the book, one for each day of the month. Ruled downwards with red lines are 24 columns. The first is for the date. The rest are:

(2) Quantity of milk
(3) Quantity of starter
(4) Temperature and acidity of milk in morning
(5) Acid test at renneting
(6) Quantity of colour
(7) Quantity of rennet
(8) Temperature rennet added
(9) Time rennet added
(10) Time curd cut
(11) Acidity at cutting
(12) Temperature of scald
(13) Time pitched
(14) Acid at pitching
(15) Time whey drawn
(16) Acidity when whey drawn

(17) Acidity on cooler (1st turn)
(18) Acidity at grinding
(19) Time of grinding
(20) Weight of curd
(21) Weight of salt
(22) Acidity from press
(23) Weight of cheese to ripening room
(24) Remarks.

In the further part of the room rather away from the vats will be the presses. And in the farms where true farmhouse cheeses are made, there are individual presses, pressing the cheeses, as you would expect, downwards[1] or vertically. In proper small farmhouse dairies three sets of cheese presses will press the cheese at different pressures for the three days they are subject to pressure, and before they go to the maturing room.

Such is the background. Now the making.

Along comes the milk from the evening milking. It is poured into the vats and held until the following morning when the morning's milk is added, together with a "starter". The main function of the starter is to produce acid in the milk and in the cheese curd.

Then comes the first of the many tests for acidity. I have watched much cheese-making carried out in many places since starting this book and do not hesitate to say that this question of checking the acidity of the curd all along the production line is the most important single operation which takes place in cheese-making.

Once you know how, the drill for testing acidity is not as tricky as it appears. This is what you need.

1 bottle of $\frac{(N)}{9}$ solution of caustic soda.
1 bottle of phenolphthalein
1 10-c.c. pipette
1 25-c.c. burette graduated to measure tenths of a centilitre.
1 glass stirring rod
1 small white porcelain dish.

[1] In larger establishments, they use *horizontal* presses, which can press six or more cheeses at once.

As to the method this is best described by culling an extract from "Farm and Creamery Cheesemaking," Bulletin No. 43 of the Ministry of Agriculture and Fisheries.

Method

In this test the acidity in the milk is neutralised by a ninth normal $\frac{(N)}{9}$ solution of caustic soda. One c.c. of this solution will neutralise 0·01 of a gramme of lactic acid. An indicator, phenolphthalein, is used. This turns pink as soon as the acid solution of milk or whey becomes alkaline by adding the caustic soda solution. The amount required is measured and the percentage of acidity calculated from this.

For the test a 25-c.c. burette graduated to measure $\frac{1}{10}$ c.c., a 10-c.c. pipette, a small white porcelain dish, a bottle from which to drop the indicator and a glass stirring rod are required. The burette is filled to the "0" mark with the caustic soda solution; 10 c.c. of the milk or whey to be tested are measured into the dish by means of the pipette and three drops of the indicator added. The solution may now be added slowly from the burette, the contents of the dish being stirred meanwhile. As the caustic-soda solution mixes with the sample a pink colour shows, but on continued stirring this disappears; solution is added until a permanent pale pink tinge is obtained and the quantity used is then read off the burette. If 2 c.c. of caustic soda solution have been used, then 0·01 × 2 grammes is the amount of lactic acid present in the 10 c.c. of milk or whey taken. Thus in 100 c.c. there would be 10 times this amount, i.e. 0·01 × 2 × 10, and the test would indicate the presence of 0·2 per cent. lactic acid. It is now known that the acidity of milk is not entirely due to the presence of free lactic acid, but the general utility of the test is in no way impaired.

After all this testing has been done (which only takes a minute), the rennet is added. This turns the cheese into an enormous junket.

You wait for a moment and then you "cut the curd" with a sort of oblong tennis racket which has stainless steel cutters running vertically down it. This you put into the curd and pull it along and it cuts the junket into oblong slivers.

After this you get another cutter, this time with the stainless steel cutters running horizontally. By plunging this into the tank and running it through the curd (both cutters are pulled through the curd both lengthwise and across the tank) you eventually cut it into tiny pieces.

Then you test and record the acidity again.

Then you "scald" the curd, by turning on the steam and letting it fill the jacketed part of the tank. Not all curds are heated to the same temperature. Friesian cows' milk, for example, will stand scalding to a higher temperature than will Shorthorn milk, which if it was heated so much would become leathery. But the temperature does not affect the quantity of the final cheese. The curd is heated from 85° F. to 102° F. In a smallish tank the heating is maintained for about forty minutes, during which time the curd is stirred continuously with a wooden contraption looking like a rake which has the prongs sticking out of both sides of the centre bar. Next the curd is "pitched". This sounds misleadingly violent, but actually the process of pitching is simply the action of *ceasing* to agitate the cooked curd with the wooden rake affair and this causes the curd to fall to the bottom of the tank.

The acidity is tested again.

Then the whey is drawn. This consists of turning a stop-cock at the bottom of the tank, and releasing the whey which rushes out along a gulley, then in pipes underground across the yard and into a tank where it is stored to feed the pigs.

At the bottom of the tank you now have a white solid mass and its likeness to a huge rubber sponge in feel as well as looks is remarkable.

This is then cut with a knife into chunks the size of a large brick and put on to pieces of strong muslin or linen which are lying on the cooler. These bricks are just piled up (with pieces of muslin interspersing each layer) until the whole looks like a huge white steak pudding, for the ends of the big piece of muslin on which the brick curds were placed are now tied up at the top. There the bundle just waits for ten, twenty, thirty minutes according (and this is most important) to the acidity of the milk. This is the point probably, where the farmhouse is able to beat the mass-produced. It isn't only that the acidity is yet again tested, but that the knowing eye can tell just by looking at the curd whether to speed up or slow down the process of expelling the last of the whey from the curd.

Anyhow after a while, the bundle is undone and the bricks are now cut into smaller bricks which go on to another piece of muslin, and the process of piling up starts all over again. When it is done, a board is placed on top of the mass and weights are placed on top. Sometimes this is all done again.

Then (and we can almost call it cheese now) comes the "grinding" or "milling" which is what it implies—a small electric grinder or mill with rotating knives which deprives the cheese of yet more whey. At this stage salt is added in the proportion of 2 lb. to 100 lb. of curd.

Then the cheese goes to the presses where it is subjected to three different pressings at increasingly high pressures for three days. Then it goes into the maturing room where it is turned first daily for a week or so, then weekly for a month and then in about six months (according to the time of year and quality of making) it is ready for eating.

But it isn't in fact as simple as that. Even the circular piece of cloth which goes on the top and bottom of the Cheddar has to be carefully chosen. Sometimes the suppliers produce cloths which have too much dressing (called "batter" in the slang of the trade), and this prevents the cheese breathing properly which in turn shows up in unpleasant black sweat marks on the surface of the cheese.

In Scotland, where labour would appear to be less scarce, and where Cheddars are called Dunlop, they have a special way of wrapping the cloth round it like a puttee wound round a man's leg.

In pre-war days the really fine old farmhouse Cheddars used to be matured not in hoops or moulds as now, but in very strong calico corsets. These are beautiful examples of the craftsman's art, immensely strong with little brass eyelets for the lacing up and with a flap behind these eyelets so placed as to prevent them from disfiguring the rind of the cheese.

When the cheeses are ready for market they will in all probability be purchased by a factor who will store them for a while before passing them on to the wholesaler. The factor's buyer (or now often a Milk Marketing Board Inspector) will grade and taste the cheeses, and for this he will use a wooden handled steel bladed contraption called sometimes a cheese-iron or a cheese-trier. What is less commonly known is that there are different shapes of triers for different cheeses.

The way they work is as follows. Imagine a piece of piping slit lengthwise down the middle, sharpened at one end and attached to a handle at the other—in all about 8 inches long. This is driven into the cheese with a sharp little jab (this to pierce the linen cloth) then afterwards more slowly and at the same time given a twist. When pulled out the trier brings with it a circular bore of cheese. This the expert looks at and, if necessary, he nicks about a third of an inch between forefinger and thumb and tastes it. Then back goes the trier with the bore of cheese and out comes the trier divested of its booty by the simple expedient of holding the thumb against the cheese as the trier is pulled out.

As for the exact types of trier here they are:
For Cheddars and Cheshires. Five designs:

(a) Blade length 5 inches with gauge $\frac{3}{4}$ inch, no taper.

(b) Blade length 5 inches, gauge $\frac{11}{16}$ inch, tapering down to $\frac{5}{8}$ inch.

(c) Blade length $4\frac{1}{2}$ inches, gauge $\frac{5}{8}$ inch, tapering down to $\frac{9}{16}$ inch.

(d) Blade length $4\frac{1}{2}$ inches, gauge $\frac{9}{16}$ inch, tapering down to $\frac{1}{2}$ inch.

(e) Blade length 6 inches, gauge $\frac{3}{4}$ inch, tapering down to $\frac{1}{2}$ inch.

Then there are three designs of soft cheese-triers:

The Caerphilly—$4\frac{1}{2}$ inch blade. Taper tauge $\frac{1}{2}$ to $\frac{3}{8}$ inch.
The Stilton (a) 6-inch blade. Taper gauge $\frac{5}{8}$ to $\frac{1}{2}$ inch. (b) 7-inch blade. Taper gauge $\frac{5}{8}$ to $\frac{1}{2}$ inch.

There is also a cheese-skewer. This is something like a 5-inch long, flat, very thin paper knife, with a groove on one side. You just jab this into the side of the cheese and a minute amount adheres to the groove.

*　　　*　　　*

After Wells the other most Cheddar-cheese-conscious town is Shepton Mallet. Here the better grocers display in their windows the following jingle:

> Come fill ye up the cider cup and drink to Cheddar Cheese,
> Good luck be with the hoof and horn,
> Good luck with flock and fleece.
>
> May the milk pail fill, the hayloft swell,
> The root crops still increase,
> May our land be crowned with plenty,
> Good temper, wealth and peace.

We said earlier in the chapter that farmhouse cheese-making was an art. In Shepton Mallet, they tell a story which indicates this. In Dorset there was a farmer who made superb cheeses: his land was by no means rich, but none the less he managed his cows well and he prospered. Then he sold his farm and bought another in the lush rich land between Glastonbury and Shepton Mallet. Here he started to make cheese again, but when he put them into shows, they never won a prize. This went on for nearly two years until he had learned the knack of different techniques necessitated by the richer milk.

A bad cheese-maker cannot make great cheese even with the finest of milk, but the finest craftsman will not produce a superb Cheddar with poor milk. This is an important point to consider when comparing the methods of a vast "creamery" or cheese-making factory and those of a small farmhouse. Remember that the milk of one cow with mastitis can ruin all the milk added to it.

Another thing that has to be watched very carefully is the milk of a cow which has had an injection of penicillin: for a day or so it will produce milk which plays havoc with cheese-making.

Cheese-making is a combination of clean cows, care and craftsmanship.

HOME-MADE SOFT CREAM CHEESE

There is no essential difference, no official demarcation, no precise dividing line between a soft cheese and a hard one. By and large, the more you cook it—like Emmental—and/or the greater the pressure you exert upon it, the harder a cheese will be.

To make your own cream cheese, all you need is a little rennet and some muslin. Here is a recipe:

Take two quarts of milk and add 2 teaspoonfuls of rennet. Put in a warm place overnight, when it will have set like a junket. Now pour this into a piece of butter muslin, tie up and hang on a hook over a basin (this doesn't help the cheese—only the floor) and leave to drip till nearly solid. That is your basic cream cheese; from there on comes the parting of the ways.

(1) You can add salt and pepper and use it as a mild sandwich spread.

(2) You can pep it up with chopped olives, anchovies and paprika and turn it into a sort of English Liptauer.

(3) You can whip in a little real cream and eat it as they do in France with castor sugar.

(4) You could have left it in the muslin bag longer, when more liquid would have drained away, more bacteria would have got at it and your cream cheese would be firmer, much more flavoury and, I think, pleasanter.

YOGHURT

Or, alternatively, Yogurt, Yaghourt, Yoghurd, Yogourt, Yaourt and eight other different spellings since it was first mentioned in the English language in 1625: "Neither do they (i.e. the Turks) eat much Milke, except it bee made sower, which they call Yoghurd."

The *Oxford English Dictionary* definition is "a sour fermented liquor made from milk, used in Turkey and other countries of the Levant". Today, it has got as far away from this as has a modern bicycle from a pennyfarthing. One modern widely read author on cookery describes it as "fairly thick, slightly acid and an agreeable substance, having health-giving properties, provided it is not laden with sugar".

The prime difference between Yoghurt cheese and other soft cheese such as Camembert, Brie and others is that the starter is a very acid one called *bacillus bulgaricus*, which gives a true yoghurt its sharp flavour.

CHAPTER III

Buying, Storing, Keeping and Serving Cheese

THE WHOLESALER

To watch the curd in the vast stainless steel tanks being cut before a Leicester is made; to look at the serried rows of some fine Stiltons—both are impressive sights.

No such interest can be evinced by a call at the wholesalers. In fact a visit to such a firm in London is remarkable less for the sight of the cheeses than the sight of vast piles of wooden slatted boxes—far more indeed than the staff need or can manage to take home for firewood. And though the premises are quite clean, there is perforce a great air of higgledy-piggledyness, owing to the fact that the cheeses coming in from the Continent, have to be unpacked, divided up and usually delivered the same day.

Again, unlike farmhouse and even factory cheese-making, there are no techniques, no old crafts, to be picked up. An accurate accounting system, good weighing machines and reliable telephonists and van driver, are all that are needed save the salesmanship needed to unload the product on to the grocer.

There is one exception. Brie is a tricky cheese to handle; some retail grocers like it riper than others, and for those that do the wholesaler must not only store it in his warehouse, but must remember to turn it carefully daily. Should this be forgotten, then the cheese will get too runny on the bottom and will remain chalky on top.

The packs the cheese come in are all dictated by the shape of the cheese to be packed. Here are some:

Brie comes to the wholesaler in twos, one on top of the other on stout straw beds and then in slatted wooden containers.

Camembert comes in slatted wooden boxes of five dozen. But this pack is dying out now and packs of twenty-four are more common.

Port Salut. These come in long wooden oblong boxes containing six cheeses. That is, two deep and three along.

Gorgonzolas come in single wicker baskets weighing 20 lb. Often, though, now, half Gorgonzolas are ordered.

Tome au Marc de Raisins. This comes in sixes in round cylindrical wooden tubs.

Goudas and Edams come in cardboard boxes—six to a box.

Emmentaler. These weigh anything from 140 to 300 lb. and the great brutes come in wooden tubs, singly naturally.

Gruyère. That is Emmentaler's more high class and racy half-brother, comes in single tubs—weight 70 lb. Actually there is a minor art in cutting these cheeses. Most grocers only want a fraction of a whole cheese, and they don't want what little they do order to be crookedly cut. So the Emmental cheese man is a comparatively important person, for he must use his cheese wire properly.

Stilton. These when delivered in England come loose, so do *Cheddars, Cheshires, Caerphillys* and the rest.

CHEESE AT YOUR GROCER

It is generally agreed that a grocer builds up his business on his provisions (as distinct from dry groceries like tea, sugar, treacle, jam, biscuits, etc.—but these again are divided up and anything slightly out of the ordinary is called "fancy"). Of these the one which really pulls the women in is bacon. There is some slight craft in cutting up bacon, with the way it is sliced and particularly in the deboning, and a good bacon man is worth a good wage.

Another provision is cheese; and it falls between many stools. In the first place it is not so very important that a trip would be made to another grocer to make a special purchase. So that though perishable it doesn't fit into the "build up the business" category.

Cleverly cut bacon can show a fair profit ratio. Not so with cheese. Here the profit is negligible, and unlike sugar and detergents, there are cutting up losses and also losses due to the surfaces drying off.

In most grocers' shops, those cheeses which are not in the ordinary run of the housewife's daily requirements, i.e. Edam, Cheddar, Cheshire, Mousetrap, are called "fancy" cheeses. Camembert, Brie, Port Salut are all such.

As usual, Brie being the greatest at its best (I do not, of course, refer to the little wedges wrapped in greaseproof and put into wooden triangular chips, but the whole "farmhouse" type on its individual mat) does need a slight knack if it is to keep well. As it ripens, the gooey part will tend to run out all over the straw and this with a little care can be prevented. It is done by getting two thin strips of wood, in length the radius of the Brie, about an inch wide, and pushing them against the open running cuts.

SERVING CHEESE IN RESTAURANTS

Fashions in running restaurants change with the age. One definite trend, for example, is for the more exclusive places to confine themselves to a quite small à la carte selection and never to vary it month in month out. No daily specials are offered or wanted. Here, too, the set or table d'hôte meal is *vieux jeu* and never seen.

Another trend is the offer of the "Assorted cheeses from the board". Gone is the Camembert 1s. 9d., Brie 2s. 3d., Gorgonzola 1s. 3d., Cheddar 1s. All are offered together (with that bitter degradation of the biscuit world "cream crackers"), at an all-in price.

Round comes a large wooden oblong board with as many cheeses on it as . . . Ah! there is the secret. It is a question of a combination of cash outlay and staff training. A really good board can only be maintained by a restaurant which is on the peak of its form: the more sorts there are the more the eye of the customer is pleased, the more often he or she selects cheese instead of a sweet, and so the turnover of fresh cheese can be maintained. After each service, i.e. lunch and dinner, the waiter in charge must pare off dry edges, generally freshen up the cheese and always scrub the board. Often the waiter serving the cheese hasn't the faintest notion of the names of the cheeses offered. This is bad staff organisation and often as much the manager's fault as that of the waiter, who should be told what the varieties are.

Alternatively, you can write out little cardboard slips and stick them with little pins on to the cheeses. This method should only be used if one has (a) someone who has a distinctive handwriting, or (b) someone who can type the names out on a piece of thin cardboard and can cut out afterwards, and (c) if it can be done frequently; greasy signs are disgusting.

From the point of view of checking and costing, the cheese board has grave disadvantages over the individually priced cheese. Clearly if your menu offers assorted cheeses, you cannot expect the waiter to wait until the guest had made a selection and then charge him 1s. if he picked on Cheddar and 2s. 9d. if he chose Tome au Marc. Theoretically you could, in practice it would mean chaos and also the customer feeling aggrieved. Your cheese board must, therefore, have one price and you must pitch this at an average charge; and so a man who takes a double portion of Munster is eating at the expense of the dieting young deb who toys with that most slimming of cheeses, Caerphilly.

CHEESE IN YOUR HOME—REFRIGERATION

Why do people decant sherry? Nine hundred and ninety-eight times in a thousand, it is because the decanter is supposed to look more elegant than the original bottle. The other two reasons are that the sherry by remaining a very long time in bottle may have thrown a crust or that you have bought a South African sherry and you want your friends to think it is Spanish.

With cheese one of the most common clichés is that they are ruined if they are put in a refrigerator. This exaggeration has grown up because of all the hundreds of foods which can be put into a refrigerator, cheese is one of those which benefit least.

A refrigerator lowers the temperature. Low temperatures mean reduced bacterial activity. To retard development of anything getting ripe or decomposing you refrigerate it. You wouldn't put potatoes in a refrigerator if you wanted the space for butter. The amount of good or harm done to a potato by being refrigerated is imperceptible. Therefore the salesmen say "never put potatoes in a fridge". Over the years, this comes to be accepted as meaning "potatoes in a fridge spoil them".

That is all about cheese and your fridge, save that if you have a Camembert which is beginning to run at 10 a.m. and you want it for supper at 8 p.m., you will put it in the fridge till 5 p.m. on a cold day and 7 p.m. on a boiling one. Crumbly cheeses do tend to dry up. They are not ruined though.

But your refrigerated cheese must be in a container. That is important.

CHEESE RIND

With all cheeses, and especially Cheddar, Cheshire, Stilton and Camembert, the nearer the rind the stronger the taste.

As to the edibility of the rind itself, here is the "low-down". Many "hard pressed" cheeses, as the firmer ones are called, have as rinds calico or linen bindings, while others have been treated with paraffin wax, charcoal and dyes. The advice is—do not consume them. We would not, for health or digestive reasons, counsel the eating of the rind of Stilton or Tome au Marc de Raisins.

This leaves the rinds of semi-soft cheeses, of which Monsieur Fromage, Pont l'Evêque, Brie and Camembert are the best examples. Here it is a matter of your digestive powers, personal taste, how long the cheese has been out of its box where it has been, and who has been handling it.

CHAPTER IV

Cheese Dishes

HOT DISHES

GET one principle straight when you are thinking of making a hot cheese dish: there are three entirely different operations and you need to decide which of these you intend to perform.

First there is the toasted cheese snack; than this nothing can be more delicious, but it can hardly be called cooking. Most cheeses having been subjected to heat, melt and then reform themselves into an elastic rubber-leather pulp. With a toasted cheese dish, therefore, the art is to get it from the fire to the plate and into the mouth with all speed; in fact toasted cheese is something which should be eaten only in the kitchen or seated round a fire.

Second comes the cheese dish where the cheese is enveloped in a hot outer casing which serves to keep it hot and in a runny state.

Third comes the dish where the cheese is worked into a sauce and so prevented from going rubbery.

The only exception to these rules is when you are cooking with a cheese which has already been subjected to considerable heat; in fact, it can almost be said that it has already been cooked.

FRANCE

Soupe à l'oignon au Fromage (onion soup with cheese). Fry your onions gently in good butter, add a dusting of flour and let it cook till it is brown. Add water (not a stock for once), salt and pepper and let it cook.

Separately put in a soup tureen thin slices of bread, then a little grated Gruyère, then slices of bread and so forth four or five layers deep. Add a few butter knobs. Next pour on the onion water. You can either leave the bits of onion floating around or take them out.

Croque-Monsieur. In between two slices of buttered bread *without* the crust, put a thin slice of Gruyère and a thin slice of ham. Bake with plenty of butter in an oven.

Camembert Fritters. Cook up in a saucepan, stirring all the while, a whole skinned Camembert, butter, salt, cayenne, nutmeg, and flour.

This brew should be solid enough to allow it to be divided up and rolled into small rissoles which are then dipped into flour and afterwards dipped into some well-whisked eggs, salt, pepper and a little olive oil. After this you fry.

Quiche au Fromage (hot open cheese flan). First make a fairly short crust flan 8 inches in diameter, and prick the bottom well. At the bottom place several thin slices of fresh (i.e. not old and dry) Gruyère. Next beat up three whole eggs with salt, pepper, nutmeg and milk and pour on top of the Gruyère. First bake it in a brisk oven to let it set, then in a slower oven to finish it off. It must be served at once. (For 3 persons as a main dish. For 6 persons as a supper snack.)

Cotelettes de Veau à la Milanaise. Cutlets *mean* cutlets —that is, a piece of veal *on* the bone, not horrid little pieces of scrag end of leg flattened out in the hope that no one will notice the sinews. Flatten out the meat part, but don't overdo this. Then dip in flour, with a whole beaten-up egg and then in a mixture of very fine breadcrumbs and grated Parmesan. Fry your veal.

Poisson à la Péruvienne. Never despise cod; it is a sign of snobbish ignorance. Cut into pieces the size of your middle finger and cook in a little rich salted milk. This should take some 20 minutes if you cook it as gently as you should, and when it is done you should thicken the liquid with grated Gruyère. Add to this mixture a handful of peeled prawns, and when you are ready to serve put the whole on a large hot plate and crown the fish with as many poached eggs as there are guests.

Pannequets au Fromage (cheese pancakes). Make three small pancakes for each person, with pepper, but with no salt.

Next make a Béchamel sauce (milk, flour, butter, veal stock, thyme and onion) and add to it half the quantity of Brie or Camembert, or Pont l'Evêque, or Gruyère or Port Salut or Saint Paulin well pounded. Put this mixture inside the pancakes, roll up, but before serving dust over fairly thickly with grated old Gruyère and brown under oven.

Pommes de Terre Mont d'Or. Boil some potatoes in their skins in salted water. Peel and mash, add salt, nutmeg, butter and beaten egg yolk and white. If the mixture is still too dry, add a little milk. Dab in irregular blobs on a tin, sprinkle liberally with grated Gruyère and put for a few moments to sizzle and brown in a hot oven.

Endives Gratinées. The private house never seems to see this delicate, trouble-rewarding vegetable properly done. The reason is that the housewife cooks it as she should cook most vegetables—namely, by boiling them quickly and serving them. But the endive should be poached first and then drained of all the vast amount of liquid which remains in the leaves and after this has been done, sautéd in a little butter or stock.

If one wishes to go one better, a little Gruyère can be grated upon the top. Put the endives thus in a brisk oven and brown.

Coquilles de Volaille à la Mornay. This is one of those dishes that our grandparents employed a well-paid cook to prepare and was one of the best things she could offer. Now people are frightened it is nothing but a cheap way of using up the old "left-overs" and so, however good it may be, it is not in favour.

Cut into thin cigarette-size slices what remains of your roast chicken. Add to this fried finely chopped mushrooms. Make a Béchamel sauce and add plenty of grated Gruyère and to this add the chicken and mushrooms. Fill your scallop shells with this mixture, dust some more cheese on top and pop under a hot grill.

Paillettes au Parmesan (cheese straws). Prepare some puff paste with $\frac{2}{3}$ lb. of butter, roll it out twelve times, dusting both the paste and the table with grated Parmesan and a little cayenne pepper, so that the pastry may absorb as much as possible of these. Then roll it into square layers of 4-inch sides, $\frac{1}{8}$ inch thick; cut these into ribbons of $\frac{1}{8}$ inch; set on buttered trays, bake in a very hot oven, and if to be used as a dinner-party savoury, serve on a napkin.

Crème frite au Fromage (hot cream cheese and rice puffs). Mix together 2 oz. of cooked creamy rice, 3 oz. flour, 2 eggs and 1 egg yolk. Dilute with milk and season with salt and nutmeg, boil and cook, stirring well. Add 3 oz. of grated Gruyère and cut into elongated flat rissoles. Roll these in beaten egg, grated cheese and breadcrumbs and fry at the last moment. (For 6 persons— recommended as a late supper dish.)

GREAT BRITAIN

The fame of the Welsh Rarebit has gone round the world. It is tried out by chefs from California to Cathay. Then it returns to the Mother Country in various guises. Actually the older form is Welsh Rabbit and in 1747 the mighty Mrs. Glasse in her famous cookery book gave what is nearly the correct recipe: "To make a Welsh-rabbit. Toast the bread on both sides, then toast the cheese on one side and with a hot iron brown the other side."

The true dish is either plain toasted cheese curd on toast or more commonly "cheese and a little butter melted and mixed together to which are added ale, cayenne pepper and salt, the whole being stirred until it is creamy and then poured over buttered toast." Thus speaks the *Oxford English Dictionary*.

Here follow three recipes for Welsh Rarebit. The first by one of the greatest French chefs of all time, the second by a famous English chef, the third by an American. My only comment is that the first, which is the most traditionally correct, tastes the least good, while the third which is furthest away, is the best.

I. Melt diced pieces of cheese in a few tablespoonfuls of pale ale and English mustard. As soon as the cheese has melted, it is poured over the pieces of buttered toast, quickly smoothed over with the flat of a knife and sprinkled with cayenne.

II. 5 oz. grated Cheshire, $\frac{1}{2}$ teaspoonful salt, 1 oz. butter, 1 oz. self-raising flour, 1 large teaspoonful dry mustard, 2 tablespoonfuls beer, 4 pinches pepper. Melt the fat, stir in the flour and mustard and beer. Put on buttered toast. Then trim the crusts and pop under a hot grill till the rarebit is golden brown and bubbling. (For 6 persons.)

III. 1 lb. American Cheddar, 3 tablespoonfuls butter, ½ teaspoonful each of salt and dry mustard and paprika and Worcestershire Sauce, 1 cup beer, 2 eggs well beaten. Use a double boiler and melt the cheese, etc. Add the beer slowly. When the mixture bubbles, stir in the eggs. Have ready lightly toasted on one side only English muffins. Pour the rarebit over each and serve. (For 12 persons.)

Hot Cheese and Bread Pudding. This recipe is to be found in a recipe book compiled by yet another great French chef and called Pudding de Fromage de Pain, obviously a translation into French from the original English. It is so simple as to appear almost impossible that it could be so delectable.

Set some thin slices of stale buttered and cheese-sprinkled bread in a fireproof dish. When the dish is three parts full, cover the top with the yolks of four eggs mixed up with chicken or veal stock and remember that ¼ pint of the liquid is just about the right amount for a pint-sized pie dish.

Next sprinkle copiously with grated Parmesan and bake in an oven. (For 6 persons.)

Cauliflower Cheese. Some vegetable flavours blend with cheese in your mouth, to form a new and pleasant taste. Others contrast in so far as when eating cheese with them, you get two entirely distinct flavours on the taste buds. In the first group are the potato and more so the cauliflower, which seems to blend with cheese in an uncanny way. In the contrasting group is cheese and asparagus so beloved by America.

Ingredients: 1 medium-sized cauliflower, finely grated cheese, breadcrumbs, milk, pepper and salt. A knob of butter.

Boil the cauliflower in a saucepan in the normal way and break it up gently or put it whole into a pie dish. Now press the cheese and breadcrumbs into the cauliflower and pour a little milk into the bottom of the pie dish. Dust the cauliflower with the knob of butter and bake in a crisp oven.

This recipe is a half-way house between a dry cauliflower *au gratin* and one with a sauce. It has the advantage that those guests who like wet food can be made as happy as those who like their food crisply dry.

AMERICA

These recipes are serious rivals to anything the Old World offers.

Zucchini and Cheese. From the Italian *zucca*, a gourd or a head; in other words, baby marrows full of flavour and in no way resembling the watery monstrosities we grow in England.

Wash the zucchini and slice. Put a layer in a casserole, then a layer of cheese and so on till you get to the top. Pour on a tin of tomato sauce which has been mixed with bread crumbs. Dot over with butter and bake in a moderate oven. (For 8 persons.)

Peppers and Cheese Italienne. This dish, so far from being the ghastly jumble it sounds like, is in fact excellent. To add that it nourishes is perhaps an understatement. The dish gets the Italian part of its name from the fact that peppers or pimentos, or capsicums, are always associated with Mediterranean seaboard countries; the walnuts and raisins are entirely American.

Take $\frac{1}{2}$ lb. of minced beef and $\frac{1}{2}$ lb. minced pork, $\frac{1}{4}$ cup each of olive oil, of seedless raisins, of shredded Cheddar, of bread-crumbs and of broken walnuts, and also 2 chopped hard-boiled eggs. Fry the meat in the olive oil for 10 minutes. Now drain away the oil and add to the meat all the other things mentioned and pound them up. Next get one green pimento per person. Cut off the top, remove the seeds and stuff with the mixture. Replace the top you cut off and secure with a cherry stick. Place in a deep baking dish, cover with a well greased piece of greaseproof paper and bake slowly. Serve with a hot rich tomato sauce. (For 8 persons.)

Cheese and Bacon Pie. Line an 8-inch pie dish with pastry dough. Boil 4 thick slices of gammon, drain and wipe dry. Put half of these cut up at the bottom of the dish on the pastry. Now put on a smearing of Camembert, then more bacon. Next beat up 3 eggs and a pinch of nutmeg, 1 tablespoonful of flour, 2 cups of milk and a tablespoonful of melted butter. Season with salt and pepper, strain and pour over the contents of the pie. Bake until the custard is set and the top nicely browned. (For 3 persons as a main dish. For 6 persons as a supper snack.)

Golden Buck. Take ½ lb. of Cheddar and stew with salt and pepper and ale in a saucepan until the mixture is smooth. Toast per person 1 slice thick rye bread and poach 1 egg. Butter the bread thickly, place the egg on top, cover with the cheese ale sauce and handsomely strew with chopped parsley. (For 6 persons.)

Baked Cheese and Tuna Noodles. Ingredients: 8 oz. noodles, 6 oz. grated cheese, 3 tablespoons flour, 3 tablespoons butter. 1 small 8 oz.-tin tunny fish. 1 cup milk. Salt, pepper, nutmeg, dry mustard.

Boil the noodles for 10 minutes. Melt butter and flour and stir in milk and then the cheese and condiments. Now throw the whole together into a pie dish and bake for 20 minutes. (For 8 persons.)

Cheeseburgers. This can be one of the finest quick hot meals you have ever had, but you are bound to make a hash of it the first time or so owing to the difficulty of preventing the minced meat from coming apart. But try again; it is worth it and incredibly cheap.

Ingredients: Take, per person, 2 oz. raw mince meat, 1 egg yolk and one segment processed cheese.

The mince meat must be lean and free from stringy bits. Bind the meat with the egg, season with salt and pepper and flatten out to the diameter of a bun and to ¼ inch thick. You need two of these. Get a slice of the cheese to fit the flattened mince meat and smear with mustard. Put the other bit of mince meat on top. Crimp the edges together and toast under a hot grill both sides. Serve on a flat dry piece of hot, not buttered, toast.

ITALY

The home of that long-keeping wonder of cheeses Parmesan, of Pizza and above all, of the all-pervading Pasta with of course grated cheese. Figure-conscious Italians have long tried to rid Italy of Pastas (*pasta*=paste, the generic word for Macaroni, Spaghetti, Vermicelli, Canelloni and a dozen and one other different flour and water shapes), but it should be remembered that the Italian, especially in the south, eats his *pasta* as a main course dish and just has a tomato salad with it.

Tortelli di Erbette (spinach). This is a speciality of the Northern Province of Parma where Parmesan cheese comes from. This recipe is for 3-4 people.

First you make a paste of ¼ lb. of flour, a teaspoonful (a little less) of salt and 2 eggs. Roll this out till it is so thin you can see the grains of the wooden board through.

Next mix up 4 oz. of cooked spinach, 1 egg, an ounce of grated Parmesan, salt and nutmeg.

Cut the paste into strips about 3 inches round. Put some of the mixture on top and then cover with another piece of paste and press down the edges.

Drop into plenty of boiling water until the *tortelli* rise to the surface. Do have a good expanse or else each bit jostles against the other and also doesn't cook.

Serve in a heated dish with knobs of butter and plenty of grated Parmesan.

Pizza Alla Napolitana (Neopolitan tart). This is one of the highlights of Italian cooking and in the last ten years has jumped the boundaries of its own province and its own country and has invaded the cuisine of the major cities of the world. Basically it is a thin tart, stuffed with all the juiciest products of the sun-baked Mediterranean; all the foods that remind you of lazing in the sun, antique remains, "pastis" and the cool water dripping over and through a sugar lump into your glass and an azure sea. But the pizza when it gets to London—Paris—Rome has to be refined and smartened up before it can be set before the tables of the rich business man, so it is emaciated and served in little individual dishes, while when it gets to an Espresso bar, it is actually nothing but stodgy pastry and tinned tomatoes. If you follow the following recipe even fairly faithfully, you will see what I mean.

Get some ordinary baker's dough (not a fancy short pastry

crust full of fat), and when it has risen, put the dough in a baking
tin which has been well moistened with olive oil. Get some large
tomatoes, skin them and chop them coarsely (not into silly little
thin slices) and spread over the bottom of the tin. Take some
black olives, stone them and dot around, also some anchovy fillets
and finally some small slices of Gruyère. Don't be too generous
with the last three things in proportion to the tomato or
you will make the pizza too strong. Sprinkle on the top a
generous amount of basil or thyme or marjoram and bake in
an oven. You must eat this particular type of pizza as soon as
it is done.

Gnocchi Alla Romana (Semolina Dumpings à la Romana).
Ingredients: $\frac{1}{4}$ lb. semolina, 6 oz. butter, $6\frac{1}{2}$ oz. of grated Parmesan cheese, 2 eggs, milk and salt.

Bring the milk to the boil. Sprinkle the semolina on top till the
mixture is fairly thick. Go on cooking and stir like mad. Let this
cool a little; now add the eggs well beaten and half of the butter
and cheese. Now roll the gnocchi into the shape of walnuts or
smaller, put in a pie dish with the rest of the butter and cheese.
Cook in a moderate oven for half an hour and serve. Don't ruin
by adding a synthetic tomato purée. (For 8 persons.)

Calzone. Make the same dough as for the Pizza Napolitana and
roll out thinly. Cut into bits $3\frac{1}{2}$ inches in diameter and put on one
side a slice of Bel Paese and also one of ham. Sprinkle with olive
oil and nutmeg. Now roll up so that you have what is in fact a
turnover, and fry in hot deep olive oil.

Ravioli. This dish, too, has spread over the world. Basically
it is a thin egg and flour paste made as for the *tortelli di
erbette*, but enveloping any finely minced meat, chicken, ham,
beef or, best of all, veal, and then boiled and then put into a
baking dish and browned in the oven with cheese sprinkled
over it.

Very good ravioli can be obtained in tins, but it is usually
embedded in a tomato sauce glue. The tip here is to take away
some of the sauce and sprinkle over your ravioli some *stravecchione* (that is the extra old and best) Parmesan.

Always try and grate your Parmesan freshly. The packet stuff is all right if you have made your own ravioli, but it isn't good enough if you are pepping up the tinned.

BELGIUM

Bruges Eggs. Hard-boil 1 egg per person. Dice finely into a saucepan and add a few shelled prawns, chopped chives, French mustard and knob of cream. Mix well and put into a fireproof dish. Sprinkle with grated cheese and brown in a quick oven.

GERMANY

Schinkennudeln (ham noodles). Ingredients for 6 people: 12 oz. flour, 5 eggs and a pinch of salt for the noodles. 8 oz. chopped cooked ham. 1 gill sour cream, 3 whole eggs, and grated Emmentaler cheese and breadcrumbs for the sauce.

Make noodles and boil in salted water, but between the making and the boiling let the paste dry for a couple of hours. Place a layer of cooked noodles in a fireproof dish. Put the ham, the cream, the yolks of egg and seasoning on the noodles. Now cover with another layer of noodles. Then top with breadcrumbs, the whites of egg and more grated Emmentaler and bake. Don't eat again for a week or stick to salads.

PORTUGAL

Fofos de Bacalhau (hot salt cod puffins). *Bacalhau* (pronunciation almost beyond the English tongue) is dried salted cod, the national food of Portugal. If you have ever smelt it drying out in the sun on the waterfront of some Portuguese fishing village, you will know what a stench can really be. But as a food, don't turn up your nose at salted cod until you have eaten it in Portugal or (if you follow the following instructions to the letter) as outlined below.

Ingredients: 1 lb. chunky salt cod, 3 eggs, 4 tablespoons flour, salt (very little), Parmesan cheese.

Soak the cod for a day, changing the water often. Boil starting with cold water and remove bones. Cut the cod into two-inch pieces. Make a batter with yolks of eggs, flour, Parmesan and water if necessary. Add the whites of eggs at the last minute stiffly beaten.

Dip the cod into the batter and fry in boiling olive oil. (For 3 persons.)

SWITZERLAND

Fondu. This rather social melted cheese and wine dish belongs to Switzerland just as roast beef belongs to England, the hors d'œuvres belong to France, porridge to Scotland and the pasta to Italy. And like these it has been borrowed by other countries with varying results, from truffles added in Italy to beer in America.

The recipe which follows is how they do it in Swiss Alpine taverns and should be good enough.

Take a fireproof earthenware dish and rub round the inside with a split clove of garlic and then pour in a half bottle of dry white wine and heat over a small solid top electric portable fire. When the wine is hot, pour in finely grated dry Gruyère, salt and pepper and cook while at the same time shaking violently. If you are doubtful of your dexterity, add a little cornflour. Bring the electric boiling ring to table with the dish, sit the guests round it and give each a fork. Have pieces of bread without the crust cut into squares the size of a walnut. Each guest dips into the fondu (which you must keep hot) and goes on and on and on.

Raclette. This dish has not gone beyond the borders of the thirteen Swiss Cantons, but in many an *auberge* they have special electric fires to make it with. Raclette is toasted cheese made usually with Valais Raclette, a cheese made specially for the purpose.

The cheese is brought to a one-bar electric fire at a side table, and when an order is given, the waiter waits till the cheese sizzles and runs his knife across the edge so that that part which has fully melted falls straight on to the waiting toast.

SPAIN

Huevos Blandos con Queso (soft eggs in cheese sauce). Strongly recommended as a hot hors d'œuvres.

Boil 1 egg per person for 4 to 5 minutes. When cool, shell, roll in a thick white cheese sauce and grated breadcrumbs. Dip in beaten egg and roll again in breadcrumbs. Fry in deep fat and serve.

Ternera con Queso (veal and cheese fritters). Ingredients: ½ lb. veal, 3 oz. grated cheese, 2 oz. grated breadcrumbs, 2 cups white sauce, 2 beaten eggs.

Cut the veal and fry. Coat the veal with the white sauce and roll in grated cheese and breadcrumbs and beaten eggs. Fry in olive oil. (For 4 persons.)

Pastel de Queso (cheese cake). Ingredients: 3 tablespoons plain flour, 8 oz. cream cheese, the rind of 2 small lemons, 2 eggs, large pinch cinnamon, ¾ lb. sugar, 3 tablespoons self-raising flour, 1 tablespoon butter.

Mix the cheese, sugar and butter in a bowl. Stir, don't beat. Add the raw eggs folded in and the ground cinnamon and lemon rind. Now add the flour and put all in a greased baking dish and bake in a moderate oven for half an hour.

COLD CHEESE DISHES

DENMARK

In Copenhagen, as all over Denmark, the smørrebrød (this means "smeared bread") reigns supreme. This is Denmark's national dish; could they but discover who invented it, they would put up a statue to him as sure as they have named one of their finest streets the Hans Andersen Boulevard. On a smørrebrød can go anything, but all the best mixtures contain one item of cheese in the conglomeration.

Broadly speaking, the Dane will use rye bread for his sandwich, and he never puts a second piece of bread on top—in other words it is always open. Rye bread has more vitamin B (the least important point these days of scientific feeding—you can pick up your vitamins in a dozen other different ways), will be better two or three days old than new, and is of a firmer and closer texture, enabling all spreading to be done with considerable force. As for butter, to watch a Dane smearing it on his bread is a sight.

The well worn advice to hungry children who have been too liberal with the preserves "take a little bread with your jam" just isn't in it.

Other tips are:

(1) When using wheaten bread toast it, as this makes the bread hold together.

(2) Only toast lightly; never let it become hard.

(3) Never put the butter on to toast when it is hot.

(4) As an alternative to butter (not a makeshift, for it is possibly better) try very well rendered down goose-dripping into which salt and pepper have been blended.

Cheese Mayonnaise. This is the basis for many an open Danish sandwich. To make the sort of mayonnaise worthy of cheese, use only best olive oil and eggs which are over two and under six days old, and see that all the white is separated from the yolk—which you use. Add to the mayonnaise grated cheese, but unless it is fairly strong, it will be useless.

If you want to eat really interesting cheese sandwiches, go to the famous Oscar Davidson Sandwich House in Copenhagen. Here you will be presented with a four-foot long piece of paper some 8 inches across which contains perhaps the largest list of sandwiches in the world. Some of these are listed below; others are old stagers used by Danish housewives for decades past.

Crisp Fried Onion, Egg, Anchovy and Cheese Mayonnaise. For this sandwich use rye bread again and always, unless I say otherwise, thickly buttered. First put on several slices of hard-boiled egg. Then the fried onion rings which are done in a shallow saucepan with hot fat, then the cheese mayonnaise and criss cross with two boned anchovy fillets.

Camembert with Veal and Meat Jelly. First put two slices of the cheese on the bread. Then cover with wafer-thin slices of veal and top up with meat jelly.

This jelly is very popular. It is so easy to make one wonders why the British housewife has not favoured it. It is also most decorative. It consists of aspic (or gelatine) into which has been put coloured meat juice. It is spread on to shallow pans so that it jells at only ¼ inch thick. These slabs can then be cut into diamonds, rounds, squares and oblongs to garnish many a Danish sandwich.

King Christian IX with Fresh Cucumber and Paprika. This is a mildish cheese with caraway seeds in it. Put this on first, then cucumber *without* all the peel removed and then liberally sprinkle with paprika.

Danish Blue with Raw Egg Yolk. The Danes are fond of this and fonder still of watching the discomforture of their English friends as they eat it for the first time with such obvious distaste.

Danish Emmental and Radishes. These go together perfectly. Use, however, German pumpernickel which is the best bread for this.

Maribo and Spiced Lard. Maribo (see Part II) is mild. The lard "lifts up" the flavour.

Potkäse and Chopped Chives. Recipe for Potkäse. This is *the* way to use up odds and ends of dry cheese. Grate them up finely and moisten them with port. Allow to stand for 24 hours, add paprika and salt and pepper only if the cheeses were exceptionally flabby. Now stir up again, for the mixture will have got drier, and put in a narrow deep earthenware mould—or better a glass jam jar. The Danes now add rum. Store in a cool place.

Having made your Potkäse, spread it on bread and liberally sprinkle with chopped chives.

Scrambled Egg and Filleted Smoked Eel with Grated Emmental Cheese. This is a refinement of not only the most popular Danish Smørrebrød, but the one which combines novelty plus delight to the foreigner. The filleted eel is cut into strips the size and thickness of a short cigarette and the scrambled egg (cold of course, cooked rather like a baked egg custard, but whatever you do, not dry and crumbly) is spread on top. This is given a dusting of grated cheese and just for colouring a bit of parsley.

AMERICA

Frozen Cheese Ring. Ingredients: 8 oz. Cheshire, 1 cup of evaporated milk, 3 tablespoons chopped chives, $\frac{1}{4}$ pint mayonnaise, $\frac{1}{2}$ cup water, salt, a large dash of paprika.

Put the cheese and the milk in a double boiler and heat till it becomes the consistency of mayonnaise. Then stir in the paprika and then put in a ring mould. When this is set, turn out and cover with lettuce leaves. Blend the chopped chives with the mayonnaise and serve separately. (For 6 persons.)

Turkey and Cheese Salad. This is the sort of odd-seeming mélange which however turns out to be superb. Take 4 oz. sliced cooked turkey, 4 oz. dried Gruyère (fresh), 2 diced large boiled potatoes, 2 small beets diced, 1 pimento, green, raw, chopped fine, 4 oz. shredded endive, 1 teaspoon chopped chives.

Mix all these carefully and cover with plenty of mayonnaise. Garnish with watercress and slices of hard-boiled egg. (For 4 persons.)

Cheese Spreads. America is the home of the cheese spread; their number is legion. Every blend has been thought of, but here are some of the more official and less startling mixtures:

Cream Cheese and Horseradish Spread. $\frac{1}{2}$ lb. cream cheese, 3 tablespoonfuls shredded Gruyère cheese, 2 tablespoons chopped parsley, 2 tablespoons grated horseradish, 1 teaspoon Worcestershire Sauce.

Blend all these ingredients into a creamy mass, making sure to use a light cream as it is necessary to get a good spreading consistency. Pack in a bowl and refrigerate.

Roquefort Cheese Spread: I. Rub 4 oz. of Roquefort through a sieve, add two tablespoons butter and blend in 1 clove garlic and 4 tablespoons prepared mustard. Serve with pumpernickel. Is this potent!

Roquefort Cheese Spread: II. Blend $\frac{1}{4}$ lb. Blue Danish with 1 tablespoon tomato catsup and 2 teaspoons finely diced spring onions. Salt to taste. Spread on thickly buttered brown bread.

Roquefort and Cream Cheese Spread. $\frac{1}{2}$ lb. Blue Danish cheese, 3 tablespoons lemon juice, $\frac{1}{2}$ teaspoon pepper, 10 oz. cream cheese, 1 tablespoon Worcestershire Sauce, 2 teaspoons dry mustard.

Beat all these ingredients well together and pack in a bowl to refrigerate. This spread will keep for weeks if well covered.

Cheese Anchovy Spread. Cream up 3 tablespoons butter with a cup of grated soft Cheddar and 1 tablespoon each tarragon vinegar, mustard and anchovy paste.

Cream Cheese Curry Spread. Dust cream cheese with curry powder.

Cream Cheese and Clam Spread. For clams you can substitute tinned oysters which you mince up with a dash of horseradish sauce and 3 oz. of cream cheese.

Bacon, Chives and Cream Cheese Spread. This one is particularly good and very suitable to the English palate. Blend 3 oz. packet cream cheese with 1 tablespoon chopped crisp bacon and a tablespoonful of chopped chives. Serve on thin slices of buttered rye bread.

Cream Cheese and Cranberry Spread. Mix 4 oz. cream cheese with $\frac{1}{3}$ cup of cranberry sauce. Add salt and serve on fingers of toast.

FRANCE

Canopy comes from the classical Latin canopeum, a net of fine gauze, or a mosquito net. But in fifteenth-century France it meant a tent or pavilion, while in Spanish and Portuguese it stood for a couch. There is thus a case for claiming that the canapé part is either what goes on top or what goes underneath. This French word for the cocktail titbit has gone into every language, but the French themselves are not good at it; the blends are too formal; they are too dainty in size.

Canapés de Fromage. Beat up ¼ lb. each of butter and grated Gruyère. Cut small round pieces of bread without the crust and lightly butter. Cover heavily with the mixture.

GREAT BRITAIN

Stilton and Celery Boats. Pound Stilton with butter in the proportion 2 cheese to 1 butter. Get some celery and wash and use only the white, very best part (you use the green ends for braised celery). Cut into pieces 1½ inches long. Stuff with the Stilton mixture.

GREECE

Cream Cheese and Fresh Smoked Cod's Roe. Unbeatable either as a first course or to put on cocktail biscuits. Get fresh smoked cods' roes and scoop the roe out of the hard skin with a teaspoon (you will take four times as long, lose your temper and leave a lot behind, if you use a knife) and pound it with equal parts of Brie or Camembert if you are feeling well off, or packet cream cheese if not. Add a good sprinkle of lemon juice and pepper, not salt. If the mixture gets a little dry, add milk or cream. The more you pound the better it tastes.

CHAPTER V

The Gastronomy of Cheese

WHEN Alexandre Balthazar Laurent Grimod de La Reynière was born in Paris on October 20th, 1758, the horrible shock he gave his mother made her wonder if it was not a punishment meted out to her, a niece of the Bishop of Orléans, in marrying someone below her class; even if he was extremely rich.

Little Grimod had deformed hands. One biographer recalls that all four fingers were shrivelled and webbed like those of a bird's claw and that to make up for their small size there extruded a gigantic thumb with a bird of prey's claw at the end of it instead of a nail. The sight of the deformity was so monstrous that his mother had the child taken away to a surgeon who covered the stumps with two iron contraptions which were then dressed over with white skin.

This infirmity made a considerable impression on young Grimod the third (his father and grandfather were both also mighty trenchermen) who, feeling that his parents were to blame, treated them callously and shockingly. He was an unpleasant child when young and his love of odd, usually cruel, practical jokes manifested itself at an early age.

For these, the iron claws came in useful. At dances he would gather a few companions round a red hot stove and explain how will power could overcome everything—even physical sensations. Like putting one's hand on a stove for instance. On went the imitation glove. Others followed. Grimod, recalls his biographer, laughed a lot.

Eventually what with his pranks, his extravagances and the way he treated his parents, these latter caused them to use the law to help them restrain him. And so according to the usage of the time in 1786 a letter of *cachet* was signed confining him "in penitence" to the monks of the Monastery of Domèvre near Nancy. Confined he may have been, but how well did not the monks feed him! Here it was that his fondness for good food began to become part of his life. After two years he was released and his gastronomic instruction was completed by a visit to his aunt, the Comtesse de Bausset, at Beziers. Round and round the best tables of the province went Grimod and "red partridges, veal for kings, melons for the gods, oysters as big as fonts, quails as fat as chickens, rabbits fed on sweet-smelling herbs, and Roquefort cheese which should be eaten on one's knees" he notes, adding happily "here we sail from indigestion to indigestion".

The Revolution disgusted him; he was a socialist at heart, but here he saw nothing but the destruction of everything that France had stood for in letters, science and art since the fourteenth century. Money was short and Grimod turned his hand to writing and that is how his famous *Almanach des Gourmands* (1803-1812) was founded.

When his parents died Grimod, being well-off, stopped writing and returned to the old Château of the Brinvilliers at Villiers-sur-Orge near Lonjumeau on the outskirts of Paris. Here it was that his bent for hoaxes was indulged to the full. For, from the top to the bottom of the castle, it was nothing but one vast joke shop or magician's cave. As soon as guests arrived and were shown into their bedroom, Grimod set to work as assiduously as a scene shifter or a puppeteer, to work the strings. Portraits stuck out their tongues, others waved their arms; thunder and lightening manifested itself while drawers of the commode came clattering to the floor, and horrific skeletons appeared at the windows. But when it was all over, always there was a feast. What feasts, too! Open table was kept just like the grand seigneurs used to in the eighteenth century and perhaps the only embarrassment experienced by the guests was to have seated at table by their sides the favourite animal of their host—a superb young pig.

Thus with his famous and almost beloved indigestion did Grimod de la Reynière live and in perfect health until into his eighty-fourth year (1838). This was the man who wrote in his famous *Almanach des Gourmands*:

VI. MAXIMS AND REFLECTIONS

—Le fromage est le bisquit des ivrognes
—Cheese is the biscuit of drunkards.

This maxim has been repeated in every cheese book that has been written and has been taken to mean that cheese is liked by people who are alcoholics, that it comes to their aid in sopping up, so to speak, the alcohol in the stomach and prevents them from passing out.

But if we read further, we find that the author meant something different. Grimod, it must be understood, not only believed in eating well and with discrimination, he believed in any trick which would help the diner eat more of what was good. Hear, first, what he has to say about the *Coup du Milieu* which can be called the *glass in the middle* or what is also known to us as a *Sorbet*.

The town of Bordeaux has given us this wonderful invention, the stroke of genius which practically means that one can partake of a second dinner. Between the roast and the entremets, that is to say towards the middle of the dinner, the doors of the dining room open and a young girl of some 18 years of age, large and well built and with handsome features, appears. Carrying in one hand a tray full of glasses and in the other a crystal decanter filled with rum from Jamaica or wine or absinthe, this Hebe makes her tour of the table. Her mission accomplished, she retires in silence. Nowadays the young lady has disappeared, but the coup du milieu remains and what a magical effect it has, for each gourmand feels after it as hungry as he did when he sat down to a meal. And now, in Paris as well as in Bordeaux, women make a great point of having this glass.

Another reflection is called "Du Fromage et Des Fromages" and continues thus:

Cheese we have already said is the biscuit of drunkards; that is, of course, the salted cheeses which, like Gruyère, Roquefort, Sassenage and Gérardmer, provoke thirst and make all pedestrian wine taste good. But between these cheeses and fresh cheeses there is such a difference that one would hardly believe that they were of the same family. The four we have quoted hold a high place among the first group and to these we can add those of Mont d'Or, Franche-comté, Marolles, and above all the cheese of Brie, one of the best that is eaten in Paris.

The cheese of Holland and two or three English types are not without merit; Parmesan is hardly used save in *ragouts*. The fresh cheeses most in demand in Paris are those of Neufchâtel in Normandie and those of Viry. In the housekeeper's room a large amount is made with a base of milk cream and sugar. But to salted cheeses must be given pride of place; alone they call back the gourmand to the bottle.

Note that last comment; it is the "gourmand" who is enticed back to the bottle, not the "drunk". That famous aphorism is mystifying. Did Grimod think of himself as a drunkard? If so, how did he manage to live to eighty-three in perfect health? To call a person a drunkard means one thing; he is a chronic alcoholic. The word "ivrogne" in French is no less severe. The other solution is fascinating, but almost certainly untenable: that the strength of the word "ivrogne" has increased in the last hundred years in just the same way as "naughty" in English has weakened. There seems to be no grounds for this theory. "Ivrogne" is "drunkard" with no reservations, from the Latin—"ebrius" (from where we get our inebriate) "drunk".

It should be made clear that the famous maxims are set out and numbered at the beginning of the *Almanach des Gourmands* and that the long maxim on cheese we have quoted is in the middle of this very disjointed book.

And so regarding the drunkard biscuit phrase which has been so much repeated, we are still left in the dark as to what Grimod really meant. But what a chance has been missed! The better maxim surely is:

"To salted cheeses alone is reserved the pre-eminence of *bringing back the gourmand to the bottle.*" The italicism is ours. They seem truly memorable words.

The rest of the paragraph gives us one or two interesting insights into what cheeses were considered gastronomically worthy 150 years ago. So the—single—Holland was in the running? That is interesting. Then come the "two or three English types". One of these was "Le Chester" as will be seen later on in this chapter. If Grimod permitted three, what were the other two? Probably Stilton and Cheddar, though this is by no means certain; Double Gloucester might have been one.

Of the French cheeses how greatly have Sassenage and Gérardmer fallen from grace. True they are still seen, but they have not found their way to the counter of the grocer's shop in every main city of the world as have Gruyère and—less so— Roquefort.

*　　　　*　　　　*

Charles Monselet was born in Nantes on April 30th, 1825, and went to Bordeaux six years later. At fifteen he was already composing verses and by the time he was thirty and had got to Paris, he was considered as the foremost dramatic critic of his time. But Monselet had had to struggle in his early days; the Revolution of 1848, for instance, had found him nearly starving. Monselet, short, fat, but distinguished-looking, was also very fond of his food. So it occurred to him that in order to be always sure of a good meal, it would not be a bad idea if he was catalogued, so to speak, in people's minds as a writer on matters gastronomic. And so from his pen poured forth a complete literature on food and drink, and much of this was in rhyme; his *Cuisinière poétique* became quite famous.

For Charles Monselet (his son André wrote an excellent book of memories of him) to have indigestion was a sign of greatness, and according to his son, he dreamed of nothing better than to die at a dining table with his fork in his hand.

What did he think of cheese as a course at a well planned dinner ? From his writing we can deduce a little.

Until the Prussians arrived in 1870, he restarted the publication of Grimod's *Almanach des Gourmands* and in it comments on omissions by the first founder. "An omission remedied" he says in one paragraph and then goes on to praise Ortolan, which he says is perhaps the greatest delicacy of all the feathered world.

But Monselet has added nothing to Grimod's words on cheese.

Earlier, in February, 1858, appeared for the first time a publication called *Gourmet* and a specimen menu is printed. Whether it is a record of a send-off dinner actually given, or a guide to housewives is not clear, but it gives us an interesting, though negative, line on cheese. First comes hors d'œuvres, then soup. Next there is a choice of salmon or turbot with oyster sauce, and/or fillets of beef or ham. Birds' nests, and lobster mayonnaise follow, and then a breather for either a Sorbet Mousseux or Punch à la Romain. Now follows: a choice of pheasant galantine or chicken and truffles or snipe. Then the entremets (asparagus or new petit pois à la Victoire, a coupe des fruits and a bombe en surprise) and finally dessert. And not a word about cheese.

But the reverse of the medal is a letter by Monselet to a friend. By this time he was one of Paris's official gourmets and he had made it a habit to post in advance a suggested menu to friends together with technical advice, whenever they asked him to dine.

MY DEAR SILVER,—The month of May is such an inadequate one for feeding. Everything is of the slenderest.

Since, however, you want some guidance, here is a choice.

> Spring Soup with poached eggs.
> Sole au gratin or langouste.
> Roast Veal and Petits Pois or young Roast Spring Chicken with Petits Pois served separately with butter.
> Vanilla rice soufflé or Crème frite or cheese à la crème.
> Fromage de Chester.

There you are my friend, get something out of this skeleton of a menu.

Yours and at 6.30,
CHARLES MCNSELET.

PS. I had nearly forgotten a few strawberries here and there to please the eyes.
Second PS. Ah! Cèpes![1] To get down to brass tacks.

So Cheshire must have been one of the three English cheeses worthy of the fine feeder.

*   *   *

In England cheese as an end course of an above average meal comfortably holds its own. This is a factual statement rather than a guess, for we have analysed one hundred and ten "Memorable Meals" listed in the quarterly journal which has now been published for the Wine and Food Society over nearly a quarter of a century. Here are the results:

Meals at which the cheese given is mentioned by name	34
Meals at which cheese is given and listed as Fromage, Fromages Assortis or Cheese	32
Meals where hot cheese savouries are listed	13

[1] It is not correct to translate Cèpes as mushrooms, for they are a different thing.

Meals where a hot cheese savoury and a cold cheese were
given   1
Meals where no cheeses served   30

     110

We have also analysed an equivalent number of banquets which took place in London, all over England, in America and Australia. The proportion is the same. The answer is that if you are going to give a good dinner, you are more likely to please your guests and do credit to the wine if you give a cheese than if you leave it out.

So much for cheese at the end of a meal; let us now consider it as a meal in itself. How odd it is that in proportion to the vast number of cheeses she produces, France should be lowest down on the scale so far as those types go which can be eaten as a main course. Brie and Camembert are wonders in their way, but you can quickly tire of them. Roquefort and Bleu d'Auvergne rival Stilton, surpass it often as a chink filler at the conclusion of a good blow-out, but their extreme saltiness rules them out on their own. Perhaps a Port Salut would fit the bill, but here again it seems too oily, too uncrumbly. Gruyère is too hard and too filling. Edam too tasteless. So inevitably—though not without some pride—we turn to England and here we can get as near as anything what we want.

Now the question arises—to what extent can one give a rattling good lunch or dinner at which the main course is plain uncooked cheese and get away with it? It should not be difficult, and it can be very good.

The cardinal rule is that your first and third courses must be hot.

Next, they must have no hint of milk, bread or flour about them, for you get all this with the centre course.

Third you don't want too many varieties of cheese in your main course. We have found out by bitter experience that it confuses the guest and puts him off.

Six are enough as follows:

1 Straightforward, viz. Cheshire or Cheddar or Caerphilly or an old Gouda.

1 Blue, viz. Stilton or Blue Wensleydale or Blue Cheshire or Roquefort or Mycella.
2 Soft creamy or semi-soft ones of which one should be well known to your guests—Brie or Camembert or Bel Paese and the other a less common one like Pont l'Evêque or Monsieur Fromage or Hablé or Port Salut.
2 as unusual as you can get them.

With this assortment you cater for the stick-in-the-mud in any category, and for the novelty seeker.
With these you don't give

(a) Potato Mayonnaise—too stodgy.
(b) Biscuits—spoils the flavour unless you include Bath Olivers.
(c) Russian salad—see Potato Mayonnaise.

You do give Lettuce salad made with garlic dressing.

Plain Cos Lettuce. Watercress. Cucumber (uncut). Radishes. Two sorts of butter, salted and unsalted.

Now for bread. There are wine and cheese charts by the score. Never a cheese and bread chart. So here goes:

With	*Give*
Gruyère	Pumpernickel
Stilton	English Farmhouse
Cheshire or Lancashire or Cheddar	Toast
Brie or Camembert . . .	Crusty French loaves
Port Salut	Rye bread
Liptauer	Poppy Seed bread
Petit Suisse or Hablé . . .	Bath Olivers or Digestive

And you should give all these breads at your cheese meal.
Here are some first courses:

Grilled red mullet, parsley butter, no vegetable.
Grilled mackerel, mustard sauce, no vegetable.
Hot oysters, Sauce Mornay, no vegetable.
Hot, stuffed-with-minced-veal, tomatoes.
Stuffed green pimentos.

Petit pois au beurre.

Hot asparagus and butter.

Then comes your cheese.

The third and it should be final course (actually it is more than all right to end with black coffee) is hard to get right, and limited. It should be light and it should have no pastry. Actually some of the above-mentioned first courses will do admirably to end with; that is the non-fish ones. Other things are scrambled egg and anchovies on fried bread. Chicken liver and bacon on toast. Walnut and bacon on toast. Hot caramel crème. Any hot stewed fruit.

With such a meal, quite excellent as it can be, great vintages are not advisable. With the first course a minor white burgundy would perhaps be a good idea, and with the cheese either Algerian, Spanish or Italian red would be preferable to an elegant and elderly claret: iced lager would be splendid.

*   *   *

To revert again to appropriateness of cheese at the end of a meal, apart from our analysis of the meals of the Wine and Food Society, there is to support it an aphorism which is even better known than that one of Grimod de la Reynière.

Born on April 1st, 1755, at Belley, Brillat-Savarin came of a family who in that part of France had for centuries taken their part in local judicial affairs. In his youth Brillat-Savarin went to school, studied literature, became a lieutenant, and especially hunted.

In fact he led the rather ordinary healthy life which most young men do. The Revolution changed that. Like others, the young man had principles, one of which incidentally was that the abolition of hanging would be a bad move for the country. Anyway, he was not on the side of the powers that be and he was banished to New York for three years, and when he came back, went into a distinguished government post to which he remained devoted till the end of his life. Brillat-Savarin was nothing if not a serious writer; two of his works, for example, were *An essay historical and critical upon duelling*, and *Fragments on judicial administration*; so when his *Physiologie du Goût* appeared, the surprise—and pleasure—it caused among his friends was great. It is a long disjointed book, greatly praised by Balzac, and in its way the only work ever written, trying to explain how the senses of taste and smell work. It contains a chapter on the history of cooking, on classical gourmandising, on appetite, thirst, the pleasures of the table, the end of the world, fasting, thinness, obesity, dreams, sleep and digestion.

The book starts with his famous *Aphorismes du Professeur* to which he attached some considerable importance, as they are subheaded: "To be read as a Prolegomenon to the work and as a permanent basis to the science."

There are twenty aphorisms in all.

A few ring a fraction oddly in our ears after a century and a quarter.

XV	One becomes a cook, one is born a roast chef.[1]
VIII	The dinner table is the only place where one is not bored during the first hour.
XVIII	He who receives his friends and does not give any personal heed as regards the meal which has been prepared for them, does not deserve to have friends.[2]

Others are:

III	The fate of nations depends on the way in which they are nourished.
VII	The pleasure of the table is of all epochs, of all environments, of all ages and of all days; it can be allied to all other pleasures and stays the last one to remain to console us for their loss.
IX	The discovery of a new dish does more for human happiness than does the discovery of a new star.
XI	The order of foods (dishes) should be from the most substantial to the lightest.
XII	The order of drinks is from the most moderate (ordinary) to the most famous and most perfumed.[3]

[1] What with automatic ovens, etc., the comment could be reversed. It is the *only one* which is truly out of date.

[2] We assume this to refer to times when there were so many majordomo type of staff available that normally a host would have no idea of the food his guests or he was getting.

[3] You can also say from the younger to the older. Only extremely rarely does the flavour of an older and seemingly frail wine get killed by following something youthful and robust.

XIII To pretend that it is not necessary to change wines is a heresy; the tongue becomes satiated; after the third glass even the finest wine only evokes an obtuse sensation.

XVII To wait too long for a latecomer is to show a lack of respect (regard) to those who are present.

IV Tell me what you eat and I will tell you what you are.[1]

It is No. XIV which concerns us:

Un dessert sans fromage est une belle à qui manque un oeil.

A dessert without cheese is like a pretty woman wanting one eye.

                ★   ★   ★

So far we have established that cheese and wine are allies. What next?

All that remains is to dilate on Wine and Cheese charts. One of the first produced is to be found in *The Art of Good Living* and certainly in print before 1938.

> Claret with Gruyère
> Burgundy with Port-Salut
> Light Tawny Port with Red Cheshire
> Oloroso with White Cheshire
> Old Vintage Port with Blue Leicester
> New Vintage Port with Roquefort.

This is a very well thought out list, though it has carried refinement a little far.

But it doesn't fall into the trap that the more recent chart-makers have tumbled into. In the past few years those in charge of Public Relations of the wine and cheese trades have realised what a "natural" these cheese charts were, and they have been coming out thick and fast. They have of course been wildly hit and miss affairs; caseous and vinous marriages based solely on how much money each had at the time as a dowry. Some horrid misfits have resulted. I, however, should not so glibly cast the first stone, for some twenty years ago, I myself produced a chart which sent Moselle to the altar with Tome au Marc de Raisins, Graves with Brie, and Claret with Tilsiter. These were calamitous errors of judgment and now after a couple of decades I proclaim a divorce.

As a general principle a mild cheese must go with a mild

[1] We have put this one after the others because it is the most quoted

wine and when most of the finer cheeses get ripe (particularly Brie, Camembert and Pont l'Evêque) they take on a superb deep tang which spoils nearly all table wines—only a mighty rough young red can stand up to it.

By and large mild British cheeses are the best partners for fine table wines.

Port and Stilton are bound by incredibly strong bonds.

A medium dry sherry is the best drink to go with great French cheeses.

Part II

CHEESES BY COUNTRIES

AMERICA

Statute No. 160,065.
Butter and cheese to be served.
*Every person, firm or corporation duly licensed to operate a hotel
or restaurant shall serve with each meal, for which a charge of
twenty-five cents or more is made, at least two-thirds of an ounce of
Wisconsin butter and two-thirds of an ounce of Wisconsin cheese.*

This remarkable law was made—and repealed—between the
two world wars, and if it isn't the hardest possible enactment to
enforce, I should like to hear of a harder one. The idea is not new,
it was tried out in Spain the same way with wine. It shows a
laudable effort on the part of governments to make the public take
to something which they feel is sound and well made.

So far as American Cheddar is concerned, Wisconsin makes
twice as much as all the other States put together. As for its Swiss
cheese output, this is so high that the State is sometimes called
Swissconsin.

We are apt to think of America, food-wise speaking, as the
home of planked steaks, salads, clams and coffee. But she is quite
a country for her own original cheeses. At least she has tried to
strike out on her own.

Incidentally, we tend to laugh at the hustle and bustle of
American business methods. We pretend that such activity does
not get them there in the long run any faster than the slower
methods of more ancient countries. What moonshine! American
officials answered my cheese queries efficiently and promptly and
she had nothing commercially to gain. With other countries, who
did no cheese business with Britain, most replies were months
late, vague and lackadaisical. Thank you, America.

The Pilgrim Fathers brought a live cow from the homeland
when they left, as well as the know-how on Cheddar cheese-
making. They managed to copy well: by 1780 American Cheddar
was being exported back to England.

Brick. One of America's genuine originals; it got its name
possibly from the fact that it is made in the shape of a brick, or
more likely, that real bricks used to be used in the pressing. It is

semi-soft and in flavour a cross between Cheddar and Limburger, being less sharp than the former and less pungent than the latter. It is softer than Cheddar and harder than Limburger. It has small eyes or holes, and has been described as "The married man's Limburger".

Colby. This is a cheese similar to Cheddar, but as it has a more open texture and contains more moisture, it doesn't keep so well.

Coon. This is a Cheddar which is cured in a special way. Ordinary Cheddars are cured at 40° to 50° F. and a humidity of 70 per cent. This cheese which is very crumbly (and also coloured to a deep chocolate brown) is cured at 55° to 70° F. and at a humidity up to 95 per cent. The taste is very tangy.

Flavoured Process Cheese. These cheeses are America's effort to break at least partially away from European tradition. Americans have also learned to copy most of the traditional cheese of the Continent—and do it well. This praise is not lightly given. I arranged for the Agricultural Department of the U.S. Embassy to fly over a selection for my gastronomic approval, which approval was indeed given in front of a representative of the Embassy. This favourable judgment sent the young man into enthusiastic praises of American process cheese into which have been blended other ingredients and he arranged for samples to be forthcoming. They arrived in neat little cellophane packets, one flavoured with pimento, another with pineapple and a third with bacon. There were six in all.

I tasted them. Soap was the article that first came to mind, and I couldn't get any taste of the flavour of the other three ingredients at all.

It occurred to me that if all America liked such stuff, it was useless to tilt against it and I should have left out all mention of process cheese but for coming across the writings of a well-known American cheese-lover, Clifton Fadiman.

The blackest shadow, of course, is cast by processed "cheese". . . .
In preparation of this solidified floor wax—often the product of emulsification with sodium citrate, sodium phosphate or rochelle salts; of steaming and frequently blending odd lots of cheese; of paralysing whatever germs might result either in loss of profit or gain of flavour—every problem but one is solved: packaging, keeping, distribution, slicing, cost. One problem alone is not solved: that of making cheese.

Give our American children the processed corpse of milk and they will grow (I dare not say mature) into processed men, all package and no character.

As for other processed plastics, remember only that the wrappings of foil are the cerements of death.

Strong words these! You may imagine that the additives mentioned above are exaggerated. Perish the thought; an official brochure on the making of processed cheese tells us that it is "made by grinding fine, and mixing together by heating and stirring, one or more cheeses of the same or two or more varieties, together with an added emulsifying agent into a homogeneous plastic mass. However, cream, Neufchâtel, cottage, creamed cottage, cooked, hard grating, semi-soft, part-skim, part-skim spiced, and skim milk cheeses are not used. Lactic, citric, acetic, or phosphoric acid or a small amount of cream, water, salt, colour and spices or flavour materials may be added. The cheese may be steamed or it may be made from smoked cheese, or so-called liquid smoke or smoke 'flavour' may be added."

Herkimer County Cheese. At one time [1840s] a popular Cheddar made in Herkimer County, N.Y. The cheeses are kept for an entire year maturing. They have no colouring added so that they remain practically white, yet the flavour is smooth, the texture crumbly. An excellent and unusual cheese.

Isigny. Very little seen now. It was intended to be a copy of Camembert, but when the final product was ready for market it tasted more like a Limburger.

Liederkranz. This cheese is a trade name for a copy of and really an improvement on, Limburger, those potent little stinkers originally made in the Province of Liège in Belgium and named after the town of Limburg where it was principally marketed. Liederkranz literally means "wreath of song" and was accidentally stumbled upon by one Emile Frey, a delicatessen keeper in the 1890s searching for a copy of the German Schlosskäse, in turn a copy of Limburger.

Liederkranz is made in a size to weigh 6 ounces, is rather perishable, is wrapped in tin foil, and is very good.

Minnesota Blue. America started to try to copy Roquefort around the end of the First World War. The main reason was that up till then the know-how of identifying, isolating and then making the blue green mould *penicillium roqueforti* was not available. Minnesota Blue is a palatable cheese, but as it is made with cow's and not with ewe's milk, and perhaps because it is matured in sandstone instead of limestone caves, the resemblance to Roquefort is a little far fetched.

Monterey. This cheese used to be called Jack. At least it was first called Monterey because it was made—about 1892—on farms in Monterey County, California. Then it became Jack for short, but now the old name is back in favour. Actually it is a Cheddar without any colouring added.

Pineapple. A hardish Cheddar cheese so called because of the shape. You will hardly ever see them, even in America, in the size and form in which they were originally made, but from 1845 to the end of the century, they were in such vogue that no American sideboard with its silver bell made to look like a pineapple was complete without one.

The cheese had its top sliced away just like a real pineapple and then you served yourself by digging in with a silver cheese scoop. The rind was hard shellacked to a golden brown pineapple colour and when finished (the cheeses were 6 lb., not the silly little 6 oz. copies of today) the shell was used to put salads in.

They were first made in 1845 in Litchfield County, Connecticut. There were also corrugations on the cheese resembling the scales on a real pineapple which came from the cheese being done up in a string basket so that, like an Italian Provolone, it could be hung up.

Sage or Vermont Sage. This is one of the wonder cheeses of America. It was originally made (as in England they make Sage Derby,) by crushing the fresh sage to get the colouration and the flavour, and adding pieces of chopped sage to appeal to the eye. Business stepped in, and a sort of sage extract was added, but instead of the chopped sage going in to delight the eye with its speckles, this effect was got by chopping up succulent green corn and putting this in, having first pressed the green juice out, which is added to the curd at the beginning of the making. Now some makers are using real sage again—they find it cheaper than the extract.

The basic cheese by the way is a Cheddar.

ARGENTINA

The Argentine specialises mainly in copying the classical Italian cheeses and copying them well.

Goya. Made in the Province of Corrientes. A hard Italian-type cheese used for grating.

AUSTRALIA

Australia does not make cheese of a truly Australian character, rather produces cheeses of types developed in the older countries, particularly those of European origin.

The copies are 90 per cent. Cheddar, with blue vein, Edam, Samsoe, and Fetta a long way behind.

AUSTRIA

Olmützer. Also called Quargel. Handkäse. Quargeln. Olmützer-Bierkäse.

The smell and also bite of these pocket-sized cheeses is proverbial. People like making vulgar remarks about them. Suffice to say that they are not moulded by any other part of the human anatomy other than the two hands. Judging by the ultimate taste, that is enough. Ripening time is around nine weeks.

Güssing. Like an American Brick cheese.

Mondseer-Schachtelkäse. Also called Mondseer and Mondseerschlosskäse. Closely related to Munster and Limburger.

BELGIUM

This country takes little pride in its own regional cheeses. From the "Service Attaché Agricole" section of the Embassy, they note at the bottom of a memorandum: "The larger part of Belgian cheese manufacture, however, consists of the types of Gouda, St. Paulin, Brie, Camembert, etc."

Herve. Perhaps Belgium's most important native cheese. It is a soft Limburger type sold in blocks 6 inches square and about 3 inches thick. Sometimes they are peppered up with herbs such as tarragon, parsley or olives. They are made in the Herve (with no accent on either 'e') country just outside Liège.

Limburger or Limbourg. This cheese was originally made in the Province of Liège. At least so the Belgian Minister of Agriculture tells me, and continues disarmingly (I translate from the French): "Perhaps it would be unwise to call its odour 'stink' if a propaganda effect is desired. That is why without doubt it would be useful to use the phrase 'something between bouquet and stink'."

Maquee. Also known as Fromage Mou. This is a soft brick-shaped cheese made from cow's milk.

Remodou. This is similar to Herve, but twice the size, with a pungent taste and very well salted. Made in the Herve country in the summer months for consumption in the winter.

BRAZIL

Queijo de Minas. A chalky cheese made in the State of Minas Gerais.

Queijo de Prato. Called after the River Plate district of the Argentine where this rather yellow copy of a Dutch Edam is made. Brazilians eat it as a dessert with guava or quince paste. This masks the flavour of the cheese.

CANADA

Cheddar. The first cheese factory was opened in Oxford County, Ontario, in 1864 and since then it has been Cheddar, Cheddar all the way. The industry reached its peak in 1904 when 1,000 factories exported 234 million pounds of STORE, BULK, CANADIAN CHEDDAR or CANADIAN CHEESE, as the product is variously called. Special brands are Black Diamond and Cherry Hill.

Actually Canadian Cheddar claims to be the only factory-made cheese in the world made from non-pasteurised milk, and it is claimed that this results in some cheeses becoming as mellow and mature as an English farmhouse. Is it safe? Yes, say the Federal Food and Drug Administration of Canada, provided (and all cheeses must be clearly dated so that inspectors can see it at a glance) the cheese is kept for ninety days.

Maclean's Imperial. Orange in colour, this is one of the strongest tasting and best of the processed cheeses of the world. Made in Toronto and sold in twenty-cent white pottery jars.

Oka. This cheese in shape resembles a Brie twice as thick but smaller in diameter, and in taste is like a Port Salut. It is made by the Trappist Monks at Oka in Quebec. See also Trappist and Port Salut.

CHILE

Queso de Vaca. Cow's milk cheese.

Queso de Cabra. Goat's milk cheese.

Queso Mantecoso "Chanco". Chile's best. Made of cream, and a copy of Port Salut.

CZECHOSLOVAKIA

Bryndza. This is a sheep's-milk cheese which in Germany is called Brinsin and in Hungary, Zips, Neusohl or Landoch.

Olomouc Hand Cheese. The same as Olmützer—see Austria.

DENMARK

"The cheese of Denmark is stark naught. In England most of it would be destroyed or sent to the prisons as unwholesome." Thus wrote Viscount Molesworth, Envoy Extraordinary to the country in the latter part of the seventeenth century. Nowadays, Denmark is unquestionably the best copier in the world of the classic cheeses of other countries. Often the copies are finer.

The industry may be said to have been started by a woman. Hanne Nielson, from a farm called Havarti, in the lovely island of New Zealand near Copenhagen, set off in the middle of the nineteenth century, to work her way through Europe to learn how cheeses were made in other countries and then returned at length to her home farm, to apply her knowledge and teach other cheese-makers.

The 1914-1918 War helped Denmark to her present unique

position. Cut off though as they were from Roquefort, Camembert, Gouda, Port Salut and Gorgonzola, the Danes were dashed if they were prepared to go without these delicacies—so the copying began.

Regarding nomenclature: if you want to understand Danish cheeses it is essential to get clearly the rather confused set-up regarding the names. Basically they are trying to establish their own names for cheeses which they have copied from other countries of the world and which they used to call by those names with the prefix "Danish".

Danablu. If in England during the war years this cheese was not sold by waiters in London restaurants five million times as a substitute for Gorgonzola, one would be surprised.

None the less it was the only blue veined cheese on British tables during those lean years and we should be grateful to Denmark for it. Actually in Denmark it used to be called Danish Roquefort and this is the copy it is meant to be, only made with cow's instead of ewe's milk. French Roquefort is a very salty cheese and incidentally is not often seen in England in its creamiest pungent condition. Officially a Danablu should have a 50 per cent fat content. When this obtains, the extreme saltiness of the cheese is offset by the creaminess and as such the flavour is quite delicious. Unfortunately, much of the Danablu shipped to the United Kingdom is less fine. Weight 5½ to 6½ lb. Diameter 8 inches. Height 4 inches.

Danbo. Used to be called Danish Steppe cheese. Belongs to the Samsoe family. Is smaller in size, weighing only 13 lb. It is about 10 inches square and 3 inches high. Similar in taste to the Samsoe.

Danish Brie. It is odd that the Danes, having created national names for their cheese copies where they have got so very close to the original, should stick to Danish Brie when this cheese has no resemblance to the shape of a French Brie and very little to the taste. This cheese is quite excellent, creamy, freely running, intriguing to the palate but it is *not* like Brie.

Danish Camembert. An excellent copy. Usually stays in a runny state longer than a French Camembert and is almost as good.

Danish Emmenthal. A good copy of Swiss Emmenthal.

Elbo. Used to be called Brød. One of the Samsoe family, but milder yet flavoursome. Square, oblong shape. Weighs 12 lb.

Esrom. This used to be called Danish Port Salut and is without doubt one of the finest most approximate copies made of any traditional cheese. No cheese is milder, yet no cheese has a more definite flavour. It is almost white in colour, soft and pliable to the tongue and with small holes in it. Actually, it keeps fresh longer than French Port Salut, maybe because of the compact sensible shape which is brick-like. Weight 1 to 3 lb., 2 inches high, 7 inches long, 4 inches wide. Experts say you should eat the rind.

Fynbo. Named after a large island situated in the heart of Denmark. It used to be called Danish Gouda. Very mild in flavour; one of the Samsoe group. Weight 15 lb., round.

Havarti. This cheese used to be called Danish Tilsit, but at an international conference held a few years ago it was agreed to change the name to Havarti in honour of the farm where Hanne Nielson lived. This is an extremely mild, bland, clean cheese, slightly acid when young, sharpish when older. Flat, round in shape and 8½ lb. in weight.

King Christian IX. This is a mild Samsoe type cheese with caraway seeds in it. When fresh and the scented seeds have only partially impregnated the cheese, the flavour is superb. When, however, it gets older and the caraway seeds have given the cheese a strong bite, it can be too much of a good thing. Insist on the fresh.

Maribo. In flavour this cheese is like a cross between an Emmenthal and a Port Salut. It is filled with many small irregularly spaced holes (in old days they said it was the holes that contained the flavour—there may be something in this), and is cartwheel in shape. Weight 26 to 30 lb. Taste mild yet very subtle.

Molbo. This used to be called Danish Edam and indeed it looks and tastes just like a Dutch Edam. Last of the Samsoe family, it is quite round and weighs 2 to 6½ lb.

Mycella. Formerly called Danish Gorgonzola. At the moment the export to Britain is about a fifteenth of that of the Danblu. An extraordinarily good copy of the traditional Gorgonzola. Fat content 50 per cent. About twice the size of the Danblu. Same shape.

Samsoe. Named after the island of Samsø in the Kattegat, this cheese is the Cheddar of the country; the national standby and the most made. It is not a copy of any other cheese; it is Denmark's own type, but it used to be called Danish Swiss just to identify it. Its flavour is not unlike Cheddar, but with the slightly sweet taste of nut kernels. Weight 30 lb., 17 inches in diameter and 4 inches high and it tastes at its best about six months old.

Smoked Caraway Cream Cheese. Not seen outside Denmark. The smell is most appetising; the taste disappointing.

Tybo. Of the Samsoe family, it used to be called Taffel. Brick shaped and rather nondescript in flavour. Weight $4\frac{1}{2}$ to $6\frac{1}{2}$ lb.

EGYPT

Domiati. This is Egypt's national cheese, but it has now burst its boundaries and is made all over the Near East. In a letter received from the Egyptian Embassy explaining its manufacture, it is spelt Damietta, so you can take your choice.

It is made from whole cow's or buffalo's milk and is a soft, white, mild, salty cheese; the salt is added right at the beginning to the milk and before renneting, which is unusual.

Although the cheese is mild when young, it is capable of being kept for a year and when this happens it darkens in colour and what a tang it acquires!

Damietta, by the way, is named after a small seaport on the Mediterranean.

Kareish. Very similar to Damietta, only the salt is added at the normal time, and the milk is skimmed.

FINLAND

This country is very proud of its Vallio, the Co-operative Butter Export Association stationed at Helsinki. It was established in 1905. Now 550 co-operative dairies are members of Vallio. To these 550, belong 64,000 farmers owning 385,000 cows. Hygiene is the order of the day and Finnish Emmenthal is the country's best copy; it is officially tested, inspected and stamped according to quality—A.1 down through A2, B.1 and B2 down to D2, which last are described as follows: "D.2 cheese are those which as far

as the holes are concerned are of the same quality as the D1
type, but have a bad smell, taste, and are over fermented; appear
to have a bulk acid fermentation or have a spongy especially
tough or raw consistency." Where these cheeses go is not
revealed.

Egg Cheese. Take 6 quarts of milk, 8 raw eggs. Add the eggs
to the starter and mix with the milk and you have egg cheese.
This was probably first done in the Province of Nyland.

FRANCE

Some books on French cheeses say the country has 200, others
300, different types of cheeses. Tourist propaganda literature
and other such things credit her with this number also. My own
researches—and being generous—give her about 70 different
sorts being made at the moment. This number represents probably as many different types as *all the rest of the world put together*,
which is not bad. It is a pity that propaganda reasons make her
puff the number so much higher.

Probably the Frenchman of modern times who has done most
to popularise French cheeses is that energetic restaurateur cum
cheese-monger, Monsieur Androuet of Rue d'Amsterdam in
Paris. In my book *Restaurant Roundabout* (1944) I was able
to describe a visit to his establishment, and to reprint his
detailed calendar of cheeses, for which there is no room in this
volume.

L'Avnis. A triangular, ewe's milk curd cheese rarely made now
and eaten entirely locally around Poitiers.

Banon. Made around Marseille in Provence, these goat's milk
cheeses are only made by the peasants and each one pretends to
possess his own secret. After making, the cheeses are wrapped in
herbs and then dipped in a bath of *eau-de-vie-de-marc*. The
cheeses then go into stone jars and in two months they are ripe.
To say that they are strong is to put it mildly.

Bergues. A St. Paulin copy made around Dunkerque, now
rarely seen.

Bleu d'Auvergne. A fairly recent cheese started in the middle
of the last century and intended as a copy of Roquefort, but made
exclusively with cow's milk. It is made in the Department of the

Auvergne south of Clermont-Ferrand which is about the most central town of France. Flavour like Roquefort, but less piquant. Output 6,000 tons a year, i.e. half Roquefort.

Bleu de Bresse. A small, rich, imitation Gorgonzola from near Lyon, about 6 inches in diameter and 2 inches high. Particularly good, and now very fashionable in Paris.

Bleu de Laqueille. Made south-west of Puy-de-Dôme area in the Bleu d'Auvergne cheese district. This cheese is also a Roquefort type, but it is drained and salted at a much higher temperature to produce a harder crust. It also has a curiously perfumed taste. Lyons gourmets love it. Faster maturing than Roquefort. Output only 1,500 tons a year.

Bleu des Causses. Very similar to Bleu d'Auvergne, but made around Bordeaux in the Gascony and Guyenne area. Like Roquefort it is matured in caves; its production is on the upgrade.

Bricquebec. There is no such cheese as Bricquebec. So at least says the priest who shows visitors round the Monastery. Here they make a St. Paulin (close copy of Port du Salut, which see) which is sold under the registered name of Providence. Briquebec is a little Normandy town and the lovely Trappist monastery is just a mile or so outside.

Brie. If Roquefort or Stilton are the Kings of cheeses, there is only one Queen—Brie, which in delicacy of taste is far superior to Camembert. But also like a woman, Brie is capricious; five times out of six, it will be dry and chalky—a sign of under-ripeness— or gummy and acrid smelling, which indicates that it has gone past full ripeness and dried up. But that sixth time! Nothing can compare.

It has been known to history for several hundreds of years. Henry IV, father of Louis XIII, was given it by Queen Margot. After Rocroi the Grand Condé demanded Brie to accompany a victory wine, but its greatest historical moment was at the Congress of Vienna when Talleyrand sent for a Brie and it won in a gastronomic competition against sixty varieties sent in by the participating countries. Indeed one French historian has gone so far as to aver that this incident brought France back into the esteem of the other European nations.

Brie is made in the Department of the Seine et Marne and

almost on the outskirts of Paris itself, to the south-east, and the three different sorts are called after three towns, Melun, Coulommiers and Meaux.

Melun. This is the strongest in flavour and takes the longest time to ripen—several weeks. It has a much more intensely perfumed taste than the other two.

Coulommiers. Eaten the youngest of the three, often "snow-white".

Meaux. Between the other two. Has a faint nut taste.

The making is similar to Camembert, but far more exacting. After the curd has been put into hoops, it goes on to straw mats. This happens more than once and each time the Brie is set down at a different angle on the straw, which gives it its criss-cross look on the rind. There are three different sizes—16, 12 and 8 inches in diameter and only 1 to 1½ inches deep.

As for the flavour, let Charles d'Orléans (1391-1465), the nephew of King Charles VI of France, and the great poet, have the last word. This is the poem he wrote to his true love:

> My sweetest heart, to you I send, lovingly chosen by me, this delicious Brie from Meaux. It will tell you that miserable through your absence I languish almost to the point of losing my appetite. That is why I send it. What a sacrifice it is for me!

Camembert. If you take the side road from Vimoutiers to Trun, you will come, after driving a few miles along beautiful twisty lanes flanked by lush fields, to a cross-roads at one corner of which is an 8-foot high square tapering stone obelisk, on which an inscription reads:

EN

L'HONNEUR

DE

MME HAREL

NEE

MARIE FONTAINE

QUI

INVENTA

LE

CAMEMBERT

Up to the right, half-way up a steepish hill, is the Commune of Camembert. To call it a hamlet, would be perhaps to exaggerate its size, for here is just a small church, with the usual tragic inevitable bronze soldier monument to men fallen in the 1914-1918 War, in the churchyard; a house for the minister; a bungalow; and just one other house. That is all. Two hundred yards away is a farmhouse where Mme. Harel is supposed to have lived, but there is no plaque to commemorate this, and, rather surprising, no Camembert or any other cheese is made there.

But back in Vimoutiers in the Department of the Orne, Marie Harel of blessed fame has had, or rather did have, and is about to have again, better treatment.

There, built into the Halle aux Toiles, was erected to her a granite monument on which she is shown with her left arm on her hip and her right encircling a massive jug which is turned sideways. She has flowing robes and on her head she wears what, with respect, can best be described as a large, elongated, inverted, tapering flower pot.

Thus, overlooking the enormous square of Vimoutiers was Madame Harel remembered until several weeks after D-Day, when the Allies reduced the best part of Vimoutiers to rubble. Madame Harel joined the holocaust, but so stout was the stone from which she was made, that she was not pulverised, but merely had her head blown off.

What to do with the battered remains was clearly a problem; Marie Fontaine was not so far gone as to deserve breaking up, but perhaps a headless Madame was not the thing to put in the new Square with its spendid Mairie, brand new Hall and incidentally its lovely old imposing church, which latter escaped the bombs. So Madame Harel was removed to another less important square in another part of Vimoutiers and there, being used as a lean-to for a concrete block to cover sewage traps, she is to this day.

But a new Madame Harel is due to appear. The Americans have paid for a new statue which, at the time I inquired, was lying in a garage awaiting a fête of sufficient importance, as one of the villagers put it, to see her installed back in her original place. It merely remains to wonder what is going to happen to the headless statue.

Now to describe the making, at least the modern making, of the cheese that started all this: Camembert.

So far as cheese is concerned, what does the word "farmhouse" mean? The accepted implication, we feel, in England and France is that the output is very small, that the cheese is made on a farm, and is given just that extra amount of individual attention which distinguishes it from, and makes it better than, the mass-produced article. Alas! If this is the case, then it is safe to affirm that for every 10,000 Camemberts made by mass-production, not more than one comes from the farmhouse.

Camembert's uniqueness lies in the type of mould (the French call it *ferment* sometimes, or *champignon*) used and the method of production.

First the milk is turned into curds and whey—just like junket it looks—and it is then ladled into the mould. What is unusual is that hardly any of the whey is drawn off; the moulds are filled with what is virtually half whey and half curd. In days gone by, these moulds were made of wood, now they are made of tinned steel, but shortly it seems likely that the big factories will turn over to plastic.

In shape these moulds are circular, $4\frac{1}{2}$ inches tall, open at both ends, perforated around the sides with some 21 tiny holes to allow the whey to drain away, and they are $4\frac{1}{4}$ inches in diameter, i.e. just that of the finished Camembert.

These moulds are then placed, in the larger factories literally by their thousands, on rush mats, which in turn stand on huge steel draining tables in area the size of several billard tables.

In order to get an even distribution of quality, the moulds are filled from three or four different tubs of whey and curd and with the first scoopful the curd is chopped up a little, so as to permit the embryo Camembert to settle evenly on the mat.

When the moulds are filled, the cheeses are given some eight hours to drain and then when sufficiently solid they are turned. This is quite a knack. At the same time as the turning is done, the turner places or drops into the mould a round piece of metal. At first we thought that this was to press the Camembert, but in fact it is only to ensure that the cheese falls down neatly and does not leave any jagged edges or stick round the mould as it falls.

The next day they start the salting. This operation is not as complicated as it sounds, for it consists of a woman holding the cheese in her left hand over a box of fine—sometimes coarse—salt, while she throws up with her right hand a *poignée* (handful) of salt on to the cheese which she rotates leaving all the surplus salt thrown up to fall back into the box. She then places the salted cheeses on wire slats, where they stay until 4 a.m. the next morning (this is in the big factories) when a male comes round and does the same operation, but salting the other side of the cheese.

Next comes the most unusual operation of all: all the cheeses are sprayed with a white liquid fungus called *penicillium candidum*, which is commercially supplied. In the smaller places it comes along in bottles and to the bottle is attached a long metal contraption with a nozzle at the end. Part of the contraption is worked up and down and the cheeses are sprayed—just like spraying roses—with the fungus. In the bigger places a larger metal canister is used and this looks for all the world like a small fire extinguisher with a pump attached.

Liquid spraying is not the only way to inoculate the cheeses with this mould, for we visited another smaller factory where the *penicillium candidum* in powder (white like fine sugar or bicarbonate of soda) is mixed in with the salt so that the impregnation takes place at salting time.

Another twenty years is bound to see mechanisation taking place; the technique of getting a specified dollop dropped into the moulds by machinery is clearly not a difficult operation, indeed why this has not been done is surprising, especially since the sloppy, wet, humid and hot temperature the women have to work in, is not pleasant.

As for the salting, mechanisation has already arrived. The machine is not perfected yet and at a vast factory outside Isigny, I had some difficulty in getting a sight of the contraption at all. Eventually, we were conducted to a huge boiler-house which is there to warm the cheeses and pasteurise the milk. Here in a corner was a simple-looking machine consisting of a conveyor belt on to which the Camemberts were put and above which was a large square box housing the salt. As the machine was not working, I assume that at a press of a button the conveyor belt went into action sending the Camemberts along under the salt box which gave forth its salt. But the guide said that the machine was not successful since it allowed fat or grease or moisture to come on the cheese, all of which were fatal since they attracted a blue fungus.

The making of Camembert has spread even in France well beyond the town of Vimoutiers and the Commune of Camembert, and now a great deal is made at Isigny, a squalid little town between Caen and Cherbourg which claims on a placard to be the "Premier Crû Laitier" of France. If output has anything to do with this boast, then there may be something in it, for at the factory we were shown over, they claimed to be making 9,000 Camemberts a day, and on my mentioning the name of another firm to whom I had an introduction, I was told that they had doubled this output. To give some idea of the size, it may be added that the room where the salt was stored (it was like going into the hottest room of a Turkish bath, for it has to be kept 100 per cent. dry), was larger than the whole of the installation used by the monks at the Abbaye of Melleray for making St. Paulin.

Cabecou. A round, flat goat's milk cheese made in the Landes district south of Bordeaux. They weigh only a few oz. each. Some three million are made yearly.

Cachat. This cheese has disappeared. It used to be made of pieces of left-over cheeses put into sandstone pots to ferment with brandy, salt, pepper and mixed herbs. From Provence.

Cancoillote. This is a funny little freak which is beginning to break the bounds of its original home, the Jura Mountains. It is a cow's milk cheese which is boiled up with white wine and butter and aromatic herbs and then packed for delivery in tin boxes. In other words you can use it as a sort of cheese spread.

Le Cantal or Le Fourme du Cantal. Called after a Département which is roughly the centre of a triangle bounded by Bordeaux-Lyons-Marseille. It is a mountainous part of the world and this cheese has here been known since Roman times. It is the nearest thing France has to the English

Cheddar, being hard and yellow. It is made with cow's milk of one only milking, needs three months to ripen and weighs from 75 to 120 lb.

Carentan. This is a town of some five thousand inhabitants half-way between Bayeux and Cherbourg and some 30 miles away from each. It is with Isigny the centre of a big Camembert industry, but as a type of its own—no.

Carré de l'Est. This merely means that it is a square cheese of the East. In other words it is Alsace-Lorraine's rival and copy of Camembert. But a good copy, square in shape with rounded corners.

Chabichou. A goat's milk cheese made around Poitiers which is dying out and rarely leaves the district. It weighs around 4 oz. only.

Chaource. A Camembert copy, but weighing nearly 1 lb. Production minute, only 12 tons yearly, eaten mostly locally. Made around the Commune of Chaource in the Champagne district.

Chavignol. Very small goat's milk cheese weighing only a couple of ounces. They are also called officially, "Crottin de Chavignol". Crottin means dung. Not a good cheese.

Chevreton. A most potent goat's milk cheese which varies in its kick according to the time of milking and the breed of goat. Feared by many and beloved by some, this cheese takes fifteen days to ripen, which is always done on rye straw mats. A hard rind forms, but the inside of the cheese (they are rectangular and weigh some 12 oz. each) is runny, soft and smooth.

Chevrotin. Don't confuse with Chevreton! The Chevrotin is a fresh goat's milk cheese eaten either normally or with sugar, rather like a *petit suisse*. These cheeses are very uncommercial and are ripened by peasants in funny little wooden cages placed on wooden poles some 4 feet off the ground. Made all around Lyons.

Le Dauphin. So called because Louis XIV, on his way to take possession of the country after the Treaty of Nimègue, was accompanied by his eldest son—Le Dauphin. They were presented with this variety of Marolles which has retained its name ever since.

This is a spiced Marolles, much sought after by lovers of fine old-wines, and is made by taking a fresh three-day old cheese from the maturing room and mixing in some chopped tarragon, powdered cloves and pepper. Then it is put back to mature. Rarely seen and only made to special order.

Dreux. Made in the Department of the Eure et Loire, this is a cow's milk cheese which used to be wrapped up in chestnut leaves.

Époisses. Named after a little Commune of the same name, south of Dijon in the celebrated Côte d'Or where the great Burgundies come from, this cheese has been going for centuries. They are tiny little round flat cheeses which weigh some 12 oz. and are 6 inches in diameter.

Fontainebleau. This is a *triple crème* cheese made in the region of the Ile-de-France which is around Paris. It is a mixture of cream and curd well frothed up. Excellent with strawberries.

Fourme d'Ambert. A cow's milk Roquefort type (and shape) cheese very much sought after and made in the Auvergne district.

Géromé. This cheese gets its name originally from the town and valley of Gérardmer, some 70 miles south of Strasbourg. Like Munster, which it resembles, it is one of the most ancient cheeses of France; it is mentioned as one of the tithes paid to the old Emperors of Germany and the Dukes of Lorraine. But, unlike Munster, production is dying out. In size and shape it is similar, but as a variation it is often flavoured with aniseed.

Gex. Also called Septmoncel or Bleu du Haut Jura. This is a cow's milk, blue veined, Roquefort type cheese made in the Jura Mountains. In shape, it is like a small millstone and it weighs around 15 lb.

Gien. Made in the Commune of Gien and Châtillon-sur-Loire near Orléans and is often a mixture of goat's and cow's milk. They are quite small, weighing under half a pound. Often they are matured with leaves as a wrapper.

Gruyère. France makes up in the French Alps a very good Gruyère. But see *Switzerland*.

Laguiole. Very like a Cantal, but made around Bordeaux. Used a lot in cooking instead of Gruyère.

Langres. This is a soft cheese rather like a Pont l'Evêque or Livarot. Weighs around 12 oz., it is named after the town of the same name, an old hill-fortress north-east of Dijon. Maturing time four months. Production is dropping rapidly which is a pity, since Langres is a very fine creamy cheese.

Levroux. A full goat's milk cheese very like a Selles-sur-Cher, made around Nevers and Bourges.

Livarot. Fortunately here at last is a cheese which is closely connected with the townlet from which it gets its name. The place has only some 2,500 inhabitants (it is 30 miles from Caen and 120 from Paris) but it is one of the least spoilt and most charming of northern France. It is in the Département of Calvados, and two miles away in the hamlet of Sainte-Marguerite-de-Viette is the Livarot cheese-making establishment of Marcel Desjardins. Establishment is the word used on purpose, for this excellent set-up is neither a farm nor is it a factory. You can see by an inspection of the circular multi-coloured label that M. Desjardins is not an ordinary performer, for part of the brightness of this label comes from reproductions of medals he has won at various agricultural shows—at Chateauroux a gold one, at Alençon a silver one and at Bordeaux and Rochefort silver again in 1897 and 1898 respectively, and finally a Mérite Agricole and Grand Diplome d'Honneur Hors Concours in Paris, 1899.

The reason that M. Desjardins can be placed in neither category is that he buys his Livarots "en blanc" and immature from local peasants and does the ripening himself.

The first day they arrive, they are salted with a coarse salt and put in the first ripening room. Then they are turned and salted again and go into another ripening room. Temperature is all-important in cheese-making and M. Desjardins has in his ripening rooms a glass panel protected with a sliding door so that he can look through and see how the cheeses are getting on without having to open the door.

The smell in one of these rooms where lie on either side mountains of ripening and browning cheeses is hard to describe. Overpowering certainly; it is like the odour of slowly rotting apples, combined with ammonia, a whiff of ripe Camembert and a soupçon of seaside ozone, or if you want to be less kind, town drains running into the sea.

A good Livarot takes longer to ripen than a Pont l'Evêque, is stronger and perhaps more subtle. The ripening takes place on the surface and there is no spraying or injecting done. Before they are sent out, these excellent little cheeses are given a final wash over and a touch of reddish-brown colouring and then are wrapped round with a split dried reed to prevent them bursting out. Generally, you will see five of these reed bands round a Livarot and that is why they have been nicknamed "Le Colonel", for in the French Army, this rank is shown by five bands or stripes on the cuff of the uniform.

Maroilles or Marolles. Made in France's most northerly Département of Flanders, chiefly around the Cantons of Avesnes, Trélon and Candrécies. It is one of France's oldest cheeses and gets its name from a famous Abbey built in the seventh century A.D. In the eleventh century an ordinance made the local villagers convert all their milk into cheeses on the eve of St. Jean-Baptiste (June 24th) and send it to the Abbaye of Maroilles.

In shape, texture and taste it is like a Pont l'Evêque, but stronger; it is at its peak from May to June and then again from September to October. Ripening time four months.

Maroilles Gris (also called Vieux Gris, Gris de Lille, Vieux Lille).

The same as Maroilles, but salted twice and really super strong. Smells slightly of ammonia and takes twice as long to mature.

Mignot. Another type of Marolles.

Monsieur Fromage. This rather fluffy, high-fat-content (60 per cent.) cheese is also called Fromage de Monsieur Fromage and Fromage Monsieur.

It is Normandy made, and is nearly always sold in tiny little round, dumpy, wooden chip boxes. Because of its high fat content, this cheese is never—when unripe—as deadly as a Camembert, but when it is in prime condition it is very fine, but not quite so fine as a perfect Camembert.

Mont d'Or. A large edition and a copy of Munster, but made to the east of Lyons near Switzerland.

Morbier. Entirely a seasonal cheese made in winter in chalets of the French Alps where there is too little milk produced to allow of it being turned into the giant Emmentalers or Gruyères. Weight around 20 lb. each. A hard cheese.

La Mothe-St.-Héray. Made of goat's milk only from September to March in the Charente, and weighs around a pound. Little seen.

Munster. This is one of France's greater cheeses and is made in the Vosges Mountains and, indeed, all over Alsace. It gets its name from the town of Munster (pop. 5,000) some 50 miles south of Strasbourg. It is made from whole cow's milk and has a fat content of nearly 45 per cent. Here are the places especially famous for it—Guebwiller, Villé, Kayserberg, and the valleys of Munster and Lapoutroie.

At present a lot of this powerful semi-hard cheese, not unlike a Pont l'Evêque and quite round in shape, 4 to 8 inches in diameter, is made almost entirely on little farms up in the mountains. There are two slightly differing ways of making: in the Munster valley they make it with a mixture of the morning and evening milk, using a commercial starter, whereas in the Lapoutroie valley they make the cheese twice a day. They also make a Munster with cummin seeds in it which is popular.

Nantais dit Curé. This is a little square or round individual cheese butter, creamy and weighing around 6 oz. It gets its name from the fact that in 1890 it was originally made by a curate. It comes from the seaport town of Nantes.

Neufchâtel. In the Département of the Seine Inférieure is a famous milk-producing district called the "Bray" country. Here is made a funny little short tube-shaped cheese called Neufchâtel. It is also made in a heart shape when it goes by the name of "Coeur". It is also called Boudon, Boudant, Gourney and Malakif. But remember it is the shape not the taste which changes.

The cheese is very white and weighs around a quarter of a pound. I do not like these cheeses.

Olivet. Alas! Here is another cheese which like the Saint Bénoit has practically disappeared. It used to be ripened by rubbing charcoal made of burnt vine plants in with the salt which was then rubbed on to the outer surface of the cheese. Then it was wrapped in walnut leaves.

Petit Suisse. This cheese was born or created about 1850. In the tiny hamlet of Auchy-en-Bray, a little commune of the Oise in the Seine Inférieure, lived a farmer's wife, Madame Héroult. Among her staff was a Swiss cowman who one day suggested to his mistress that before the malaxation of the curd took place, it would be a good idea to blend in a little fresh cream. The advice given by the "little Swiss" was followed, and thus was born the cheese.

This cheese is one of the softest, fluffiest there is. It is packed in small cylinders with a little white paper vest round it; some people like to sprinkle their Petit Suisses with fine sugar and eat them with strawberries. They are also excellent with digestive biscuits.

Picodon. Every Picodon will be different. They are made by shepherds in the Haute Savoie. They are of goat's milk, very soft, take three months to ripen and this is done in sandstone pots. The word comes from patois "pico", meaning to prick.

Pithiviers au Foin. Almost extinct. In shape it was that of a small Brie (often called a Coulommiers) and before it was sent out was sprinkled with a few strands of hay.

Pont l'Evêque. The tiny town of Pont l'Evêque in the Département of Calvados has earned its red circle in, or on, map 55 of the Michelin Guide to France. This means that during the D-Day invasions the *localité* was *gravement endommagée*, that is badly knocked about, but none the less, they did not hit the attractive Hôtel Lion d'Or, which has one of the Guide Michelin's single stars, meaning that you can get "a good meal in its class". At the Lion d'Or, they will give you *Bouchée Deauvillaise, Terrine Maison* and *Poulet à l'Estragon* after which, washed down with the excellent local cider and a glass of calvados, you can start looking for the cheese which gets its name from the tiny town.

So far as keeping time is concerned (and almost without exception, the longer a cheese keeps, the more pungent it becomes), Pont l'Evêque lies about mid-way between the other two greats of the Pays d'Auge, as this district is called, and from the day of making until the time it leaves its first home, some fifteen to twenty-four days elapse. Unlike the other two, Pont l'Evêque is sold in square (not round) wooden chips and the *matière grasse* goes from 40 per cent. to 45 per cent.

Unlike Camembert the fungus is not put on to or into the mould artificially, but lies in the walls and on the ceiling of the place where it is matured.

Port Salut or Port du Salut. Laval, population 34,000 souls, is, thank heaven, a town on the road to nowhere. Le Mans is 50 miles away so that it gets no overflow from the twenty-four hours race. It is too far away from the seaside resorts of Normandy and Brittany to attract day trippers and it is just too far west to be of any use as a stopping place for those motoring from Calais to the South of France.

If this charming town with the River Mayenne running through its centre and with its absence of "English Spoken" and *"Waffles à toutes heures"* is tucked away, how shall one describe the Trappist Monastery in the Commune at Entrammes, 6 miles to the south? Suffice to say that here is peace indeed; peace in which to pray and peace in which to make fine cheese.

In the beginning of the ninth century the road from Rennes to Le Mans passed through Entrammes instead of Laval and crossed the River Mayenne just here; the boats which plied up and down the river also stopped at a spot which was called Port Ringeard.

Just by here in 1233 was founded a priory of the monks of Sainte Geneviève, who remained until the Revolution when the priory was suppressed and sold for the benefit of the nation.

In 1815 a band of Trappist monks returning from exile were installed in the ancient Port Ringeard priory and the place was henceforth called "l'Abbaye de Notre-Dame de Port-du-Salut" loosely translated as the Port of Safety. What is not so generally known is that these monks had passed their exile in Switzerland, home of Gruyère-making from milk of the high mountains.

At first the monks had twelve cows and the cheeses they made were for their own consumption; they perhaps combined the technique learned in Switzerland with that of making a cheese from lowland milk. At any rate it was good, and one day the

Reverend Father gave a present of one to a neighbour. It was found to be excellent; some local inhabitants called and, according to manuscripts in the monastery said, "If the R.P. Abbé made more of these cheeses we would gladly give him our custom."

"This," continues the manuscript, "was the start of the cheese business, dating back to 1817."

In 1873 Port du Salut cheese made its first appearance on Parisian tables and this again according to manuscripts at the Abbey is how:

The Reverend Father Dom Henri left Port du Salut on the September 10th 1873 to attend an Ecclesiastical Conference. In Paris he stopped at the house of M. Mauget, 13 rue Cardinal Lemoine, and with this worthy merchant he was able to place his confidence. M. Mauget was entrusted with the selling of our cheese at a low price to bring us in a modest profit. Three times a week we sent up supplies, a certain vogue for these cheeses started and everyone rushed to buy them. So much so that as soon as the cheeses reached M. Mauget, he put up a sign saying "cheeses arrived" and instantly all the customers flocked to buy so that in less than an hour it was all sold.

By 1878, the cheese was so well known that they decided to register the name at the Tribunal de Commerce in Laval and this was renewed on June 15th, 1927.

Now for a mystery. Is Port du Salut a different cheese from Port Salut, or the same? Listen first to a French book called *Fromages de France*, printed in Tours in 1953:

Le Port Salut. In 1909, a commercial cheese-maker impressed, doubtless, by the qualities of Port du Salut made plans to set up a similar manufacture in a part of France at some considerable distance from the original place of origin. To this end he entered into business relationship with the Trappistes of Entrammes, which resulted in the latter agreeing to send several priests to make the cheeses at the new place. The cheese which resulted was called Port Salut.

At the end of a certain time, for personal reasons, the priests had to abandon this growing industry and return to Entrammes. However that may be, the name of Port Salut if not perhaps the cheese was created, it was going and . . . has become public property (*est tombé dans le domaine public*). Port Salut is now made in every corner of France.

Port Salut is, in fact a copy of its ancestor Le Port du Salut.

Le Saint-Paulin, a close cousin (*voisin*) of Port Salut from which it derives is a milk cheese of an average weight of 1 Kg.500 (about 3 lb.), made more or less all over France. The technique of the making differs from that of former "Port Salut" in the absence of heating and by salting the curd.

In support of the view that Port du Salut and Port Salut are identical, I can cite my own visit to the Abbaye d'Entrammes, where I conversed with the lay manager of the cheese department and also saw one of the priests.

There were large vats, round and curved at the bottom and lined with copper, in which the milk is partially heated; the manager drew my attention to the fact that these vats are of the same design as those used in making Gruyère in Switzerland, while in the making of St. Paulin the vats are oblong and square bottomed.

Then I was taken to the ripening rooms, in arched cellars five hundred years old in a courtyard surrounding the monastery. An impressive sight; it was a pity that the women of the party were not allowed entrance. Here the humidity is between 80 and 90 per cent., maintained not by a humidifier as in most establishments, but by the simple process of leaving large pools of water lying about on the brick floor.

These cheeses take some thirty days to ripen and from here go literally all over the world.

As for names, the manager said that Port Salut was nothing but a contraction of Port du Salut which had come about because it was easier to say.

He then stated that a court case had [I think, in 1936] given to the Abbaye d'Entrammes the sole right both to Port Salut and Port du Salut.

Had we to rely on this, however, one could say that these statements were due to either loyalty on the part of the manager or possibly to misunderstanding on mine; but we were then handed a set of the Abbaye's labels. There are two sizes for the smaller and the larger cheeses. There are also two grades—the 50 per cent. *matière grasse* and the 40 per cent. Across all these labels is over-printed a bright dominant coloured (green 50 per cent., red 40 per cent.) band which says

> Propriété exclusive des Marques déposées
> PORT SALUT ET PORT DU SALUT
> Fromage au fermants lactiques naturels

That this is the case would appear to be borne out by a visit to another Trappist Monastery at Bricquebec in Normandy. Here they make cheeses on a much larger scale than at the Abbaye Melleray. A priest showed us round and explained that they were not allowed to call their cheese Port Salut and that they called it St. Paulin, but that to protect this name they had registered the name "Providence".

In taste a rich ripe Port du Salut is one of the best all-purpose cheeses of France. In flavour, it is a cross between a Bel Paese and a Camembert and in texture it is much nearer the former. By "all-purpose" we imply that it is sufficiently mild to suit all palates and to go with all wines and also of a texture to be consumed in fair quantities, and yet it has a sufficiently strong tang to make it acceptable as a *bonne bouche* at the end of a serious meal.

But that which the monks gained in getting Port Salut and Port du Salut as their own registered trade mark, they have lost in one other direction. Daily a thousand St. Paulins are sold in the shops to every one of the other, and so as the years pass a very real danger will crop up that Port Salut will become a cheese unknown to a younger generation.

What a tragic turn of fate it would be if the monks at Entrammes were obliged to change their coloured bands and to state that what they made was a perfect copy of St. Paulin!

Pouligny-St.-Pierre. The same as Levroux only of a different shape.

Le Quart. A miniature Maroilles.

Reblochon. A great cheese, a copy of Port Salut, but made in the Savoie.

Les Riceys. Also called Le Ricey Cendré, since the cheese is ripened with a coat of charcoal. Made formerly around the Marne, the production is now almost non-existent.

Rigottes. Tiny little, round, soft, goat's plus cow's milk cheeses made in the vicinity of Lyons.

Rocroi. Tiny little, soft, white, flat, circular cheese made in the Marne in the north-east of France by peasants. Production very small.

Rollot. A Camembert type of cheese with a history, made in Flanders, but now hardly ever seen. One May Day in 1678 Louis XIV stopped at Orvillers, was given a Rollot for lunch by one Debources and he liked it so much that he made the man "maître fromager" on the spot, with a pension of 600 livres per year, to be transmitted to his descendants.

Roquefort. How "King" Roquefort came to be discovered is unknown. Like the tale of the first wine being made when a cave man returned to find his crushed grapes had fermented, the legend as to how Roquefort first appeared may well be true.

A shepherd leading his flock of sheep out to pasture among the rocky arid slopes of the Causses hills, left a *fromageon* (a soft cheese of sheep's milk) lying against a huge hunk of bread in a crevice to pick up later for his meal. But he got lost and returned so long after that the rustic repast as such had disappeared and instead there was an unctuous mass of food covered with a greenish mildew. None the less, he tried this curious mixture and found it so good and so rich that he started placing further unripe cheeses next to further hunks of bread—Roquefort was born.

Pliny praised this cheese in the first century A.D., and then in the eighth century the monks of St. Gall, who were Charlemagne's hosts, found him picking the green bits out and they told him he was wasting the best part. The King retasted it, found they were correct; and so ordered a consignment yearly for Aix-la-Chapelle, stipulating that they should all be cut in half so that he could be sure that the blue veins were there.

More officially, perhaps, it enters into history in A.D. 1060, when the archives of the monastery of Conques record the gift of two cheeses furnished annually by each of the caves in the district.

Casanova has a word, too, about it. In 1757 he writes:

As quick as a hart (*leste comme une biche*) she covered a little table, set up two places and set forth all she had: it was a delicious Roquefort cheese and an excellent glazed ham. Oh! what wonderful dishes Chambertin and Roquefort are to restore love, and also to bring to maturity a growing love.

In 1407, Charles VI of France, by letters patent, granted to the inhabitants of Roquefort the monopoly of the ripening of Roquefort as it was made "from time immemorial in the caves of the said village which is so poor that it can grow neither root of vine nor ears of barley".

From then on and almost regularly twice a century did this fabulous ewe's milk cheese become protected and defined.

"NOTICE: from the Sovereign Court of Parliament of Toulouse. It is expressly forbidden to travellers, merchants and others of whatever status who have bought cheeses from the neighbouring caves and places in the neighbourhood of Roquefort to sell them either wholesale or retail as genuine Roquefort cheeses, under a penalty of a fine of a thousand pounds."

This was a promulgation of 1550 and again of January 31st, 1785.

Gradually the popularity of the district caused the area wherein Roquefort could legally be made to be widened and widened until now it has spread to almost the whole of the Causses.

The Causses are a series of arid chalky plateaux south of the Massif Central, and perhaps the most infertile part of all France. Here in these 6,000 square miles live a half million peasants and it would be a sad day for many of them if Roquefort should lose its popularity. For this cheese, being made solely of ewe's milk, supports indirectly other industries, such as glove-making and wool. And only sheep could thrive on such barren land. Roquefort-making, true, has spread to other parts of France, and to Corsica, but the industry of rearing ewes which bear the right sort of milk is a large one and solely confined to the Causses. If anything happened to the makers of Roquefort, 130,000 agricultural workers would suffer.

To make Roquefort, first the ewe's milk is heated and then set, and then after a coagulation period of two hours the curd is cut and the free whey is removed and the curd is then transferred on to a cloth to drain. Next it is put into hoops some $7\frac{1}{2}$ inches in diameter and 6 inches deep with perforated holes at the side. So far it is much the same as in making other cheeses, but now comes an important difference, for the scooping of the curd into these moulds is done in three or four stages and between each scoop is sprinkled a dry blue mould powder which gives the cheese its veins.

This powder is *penicillium roqueforti* a variety of *penicillium glaucum* and is now commercially made by inoculating bread made of half wheat and half rye flours with the original mould. Left in a damp room after six weeks, the loaves become entirely covered with the blue powder. Then they are taken elsewhere and dried in a hot room and thoroughly ground and sifted and packed ready to go to the cheese-makers.

Then the ripening. It is the huge natural caves that do it (though they have dug others recently). These are quite a tourists' draw in the little village of Roquefort, and are recommended as worth a visit by the Guide Michelin.

Here the temperature is low, but the humidity is high and there is also a rapidly changing current of air running through. This permits the cheese to ripen (they are more heavily salted than almost any other cheese, which also prevents unwanted micro-organisms from growing) slowly and without the wrong sort of fungi appearing on the surface.

It is claimed that ewe's milk is the richest in fat content, in casein and minerals. A true Roquefort—and at a world conference at Stresa in 1951 the contracting countries agreed that the word Roquefort was a geographical definition exclusively reserved to cheeses of the Causses area—is very creamy, very pungent and very salty. I however find it too strong to be considered as fine as Stilton.

St. Benoit. See *Olivet*.

Saint Marcellin. Famous little cheeses made in the Savoie district weighing about six to the pound. They are very soft, made just of drained milk slightly salted. No heating, no kneading, no pressing.

Sainte-Maure. This is a cheese from the Touraine and more particularly from the Cantons of Sainte-Maure and Loches in the Département of the Indre et Loire. It is a goat's milk cheese in the shape of an elongated cylinder made somewhat on the lines of a Camembert. It is recommended as a good accompaniment to the wines of Vouvray.

Saint Nectaire. This cheese has a good sales talk attached to it.

It is made in the Auvergne district around the old town of Clermont-Ferrand from the milk of Salers cows. The cheeses are matured on rye straw mats and in fresh damp caves as picturesque as can be, which used to be used for wine. Only 1,500 tons of the cheese (it is like a Port Salut; each weighs about 20 oz.) are made a year and Parisian gourmets will go to any trouble to procure one (they are only made on local farms).

Saint Paulin. St. Paulin and Port du Salut are to all intents and purposes the same cheese. One can fairly call it the cheese of monasteries of the north-west of France.

These cheeses are made by the monks themselves and a remarkable life they lead, one of work and prayer—little else.

One of these monasteries is the Abbaye de Melleraye, south of Laval. The church was started in 1143 and consecrated on August 7th, 1183. Here is their daily timetable:

2 a.m.	get up
2.30 to 5.30	public and private prayers
5.30 to 7.45	breakfast and chapel
7.45 to 10.45	work
10.45 to 11.30	free, personal prayers
11.30 to 1.30	dinner, free
1.30 to 3.30	work
3.30 to 4.45	free
4.45 to 5.30	vespers
5.30 to 6.10	collation, free
6.10 to 7.0	lecture
7 p.m.	retreat

The monks here were expelled in 1794 and found a haven at Lulworth in Dorsetshire. Again in 1901 they were expelled and came to England a second time.

At Melleraye, the monks are nearly self-sufficient. They have their own herd of cows, with a modern electrical milking installation; it looks somewhat bizarre to see a priest in his long flowing black and white robes (the "brothers" in black and brown are of a less high order and do far fewer hours of prayer) milking the cows whose names are all neatly stencilled above the animal—Grenue; Gageure; Banquise; Diabète.

From these beasts comes the milk and the butter used to sustain the monks. No meat is eaten save when one of them is ill and only the minimum milk is allocated for personal consumption (anyway they drink none from September 14th to Easter of the following year), leaving the rest to be made into St. Paulin which is sold, the proceeds going towards the upkeep of the monastery.

The place where the St. Paulin is made might be thought primitive, but is scrupulously clean. In one corner is an ordinary copper boiler where two-thirds full milk and one-third skim milk is heated to 32° C. This is done twice, then the whey is drained away and the curd put into moulds and wrapped with a little linen cloth.

Next comes the pressing. This is done on a very old-fashioned wooden press and by means of a weight suspended from an iron bar above the press. On this bar are six notches and as the pressure is to be increased so the weight is moved notch by notch outwards along the iron bar.

The taste of these little cheeses is almost exactly the same as that of Port du Salut.

Sassenage. A blue veined cheese like Gex. Weighs either 1 lb. or 4½ lb. (there are two shapes). Made in the Department of the Isère.

Selles sur Cher. Goat's milk cheese made in the valley of the Cher, South of Orléans.

Septmoncel. See *Gex*. It is round and flat and made and matured in sandstone pots and weighs 1 lb. Rubbed with salt and charcoal. Popular in Paris. Rather strong.

Sorbais. Another type of Marolles.

Soumaintrain. Yearly production tiny, only 18 tons. Made in the Communes of Beugnon, Neuvy, Santour, and Soumaintrain in the Département of the Aube, which is in turn a part of a larger area called Champagne. This is a semi-hard cheese like a Munster.

Tome au Marc de Raisins. Also called *Tome au Marc* and *Tome de Raisins*. This cheese fascinates many people; it is also very good. It is white, rather waxy, extremely solid. It is made in the shape of a flat cylinder or tiny millstone, each cheese weighing around 3½ lb. What gives it its distinction is that the rind is made of dried pressed grape skins and grape kernels. The cheese is excellent. Made in the Savoie.

Tome de Savoie. Same as *Tome de Raisins*.

Vacherin des Beauges. This is probably France's rarest great cheese which is still made. By this I mean that by descriptions of cheese now extinct there may have been better ones than Vacherin des Beauges and that many of the great cheeses (Brie, Camembert, Roquefort, etc.) made in big quantities are as good, but this one lies between these two poles.

It is made with full cow's milk and only from October to December. The reason is that during the rest of the year the beasts graze on *alpage* (high-up mountain grass) and from this a modest cheese is made. But in October they start on *regrain* which is second crop hay. Down goes their milk yield, but up goes the butter fat content.

These Vacherins are the shape of a tiny millstone and weigh about 2½ lb. and they take three months to ripen. The rind is firm, but the inside is like the most runny Camembert ever seen. You eat and enjoy Vacherin des Beauges with a spoon.

Valençay. Identical with a Levroux only larger.

Vendôme. Made by a very small number of producers in the Valley of the Loire near Vendôme. It is ripened in charcoal and can be occasionally picked up in Paris and Blois.

Villebarou. Made in the Communes of Marolles and Saint-Denis-sur-Loire at Villebarou. The cheeses weigh about 1 lb. each, are about 8 inches in diameter and a good inch high. You can make three such cheeses from one gallon of milk. They are soft, mildly salted, something like a cross between a Camembert and a Port Salut. Formerly they were wrapped in plane tree leaves. Most of them are now sold on Saturdays in the market square at Blois.

GERMANY

The Allgau is to Germany what Cheshire and Somerset are to England, Normandy is to France, the Lombardy Plains are to Italy and Wisconsin to the U.S.A., namely, her dairy-making and cheese producing centre. Allgau is in Bavaria, on the very borders of Switzerland and Austria.

Germany has not got as many different varieties as some text books make them appear to have. A second look at some of their rather imposing names reveals too many "Castles", "Hands", "Whites", "Backs" and such like, and not nearly enough regions.

Aber. A semi-soft ewe's milk cheese made in Bohemia.

Allgauer Bergkäse. Also called *Allgauer Rundkäse* and *Allgauer Emmental*. This is a German copy of Swiss Emmental and since this lush district runs right down into the Swiss valley of the Emme, it is not surprising that they are highly prized.

Before World War I, there was quite a cult of "vintage" Allgau Emmental. Rich noblemen would buy all they could get, leave them to be stored in the caves in the district, and then have them shipped to their homes when perfection was reached.

Allgauer Rahmkäse. Rather like Limburger, but milder. Often flavoured with caraway, but, with or without, a great cheese.

Altenburger. A soft goat's milk cheese made in Thüringia in central Germany.

Backsteiner. This just means Brick and is a sort of Limburger-Romadur type cheese.

Bierkäse. Yes, sometimes they actually pop a certain small round cheese *into* a tankard of Munich beer and when it dissolves, they drink it.

Brandkäse. Each cheese weighs about 6 oz. only, and while the ripening process is on, the rind is either moistened with beer or the cheeses are ripened in disused beer kegs, or both.

Glumse. A West Prussian cottage cheese.

Harzkäse. Made in the Harz Mountains. A tiny soft, hand cheese.

Holsteiner. Originally made in the turbulent Province of Schleswig-Holstein. The cheeses weigh from 9 to 15 lb. and are subjected to considerable pressure. It is a skim-milk cheese to which fresh butter-milk is added.

Koppen. So called because it is made in a cup-shaped mould. Flavour: pungent, slightly smoky.

Limburger. See Belgium for origins, but in spite of that this cheese, made chiefly in the Allgau, has been made so extensively in Germany that it is to some extent considered the leading German national cheese. It is what is called a surface-ripened cheese and ripeness is the operative word.

Tilsiter. Very Germanic. It is rather like a Port du Salut even to the small holes, but stronger; in size one of the largest cheeses made anywhere in the world. An excellent, downright, toothsome, full-bodied cheese. The town of Tilsit is in the old East Prussia, almost on the borders of Lithuania.

Westphalia Sauer Milch. A wonderful cheese! Where it is well made and kneaded by hand and the right amount of butter, egg yolk, pepper and caraway seed added, and when it has ripened —dare we say putrified?—just the correct amount, it makes a superlative spread.

GREAT BRITAIN

Blue Vinny. This cheese is sometimes called Dorset Blue and very occasionally Blue Veiny. Almost certainly Vinny is not a corruption of veins, but is direct from an obsolete Old English word meaning to become mildewed. The word is a dialect variation of Fenny or Finny, which in turn comes direct from the old English word *fyniz*, meaning mould.

This cheese has fascinated writers on the subject of cheeses for the past twenty-five years. It is certainly the rarest of the genuinely district types left in England. Because of this it is always made out to be far better in taste than it really is. It can never be a great cheese, because it is made with skimmed milk. To say that it gets very hard is a gross understatement. The cheeses (about the size of a Stilton) turn into granite. They even say that a train was once run using Blue Vinneys instead of real wheels. When fresh the cheese is rather dry and crumbly.

Caerphilly. The population of this Glamorgan town is 36,900 and it is seven miles from Cardiff. Its one pathetic little claim to fame (apart perhaps from Caerphilly Castle, that mighty stronghold of Gilbert de Clun) could be said to be that not one shop in the entire place specialises in selling the cheese which takes its name from the town.

The cheese is white in colour, rather crumbly, not a long keeper (maturing time is three weeks) but has the property of being perhaps the most easily digested cheese there is, and certainly the most so of all English cheeses. This is why it is so popular with the Welsh miners in the district, for they can consume great quantities of it and still do a day's work.

Apart from being crumbly, the cheeses lack the elasticity of Cheddar. They are made in a flat circular shape 9 inches in diameter and $2\frac{1}{2}$ to $3\frac{1}{2}$ inches thick and weigh about 8 lb. They have been copied in other parts of England, mainly in Leicestershire, but that is recently; in Wales they have been in existence for a period beyond memory.

The thickness of about 3 inches is said to have been originally chosen so that local miners could hold a slice between finger and thumb and eat it while still "on the job" without getting coal-dust on the cheese itself.

Cambridge. This cheese is quite rare. Its existence, however, is or was undoubted, for it certainly used, around 1934-1938, to be made in a little village not a dozen miles from the Cathedral City of Ely. Its shape was that of a small brick, dented on the top, and in colour and texture was of alternate layers of firm snowy whiteness and soft pale buff coloured cream. Each cheese was seated on a little mat of spotless straw.

Cheshire. Almost certainly Cheshire is the oldest individually known cheese of Great Britain, and it was being eaten long before King Alfred was having trouble with his cakes.

This cheese is, oddly enough, usually called Chester on the Continent after the ancient Roman town of that name in the County of Cheshire; but the true cheese-making headquarters of the district is the town of Whitchurch (pop. 7,000), twenty miles south of Chester. The town is also near the salt mining town of Northwich where the steps of some of the houses have already subsided because of the salt erosion; there is little doubt that the saltiness of the surrounding meadows may have something to do with the special flavour which Cheshire possesses.

Salt plays an extremely important part in the making of all cheeses. Stilton, Wensleydale, Cheddar, Leicester, Lancashire, Caerphilly and many others of this type all have salt added to the curd at the rate of roughly 2 to 3½ lb. of salt to 100 of the curd. Camembert, Port Salut, Pont l'Evêque, Roquefort, Bleu d'Auvergne, Edam and others, have it so rubbed into their outer skin in the making that they absorb just as much as those cheeses which have had it added to the curd.

Actually the salt added to Cheshire varies, because even now (one is always in this book talking of the farmhouse product and not the factory affair) the few true Cheshire cheese farmer enthusiasts, employ three slightly differing methods of manufacture according to the time of the year:

(i) The *Early Ripening*. This is a soft Cheshire made in the non-flush times of the year, not pressed very hard and sold locally. Into this goes just under 2 lb. of salt to 100 lb. of curd.

(ii) The *Medium Ripening*. This is made in May, June and September. It is ready for eating six weeks after making. More whey is run off than for the Early Ripener and it is subjected to greater pressure. Over 2½ lb. of salt goes into 100 lb. of curd.

(iii) *Long Keeping Cheshire*. Made only in July and August. Ready for sale four months after making, but can be kept for a year. Greater pressure is exerted in squeezing out the whey, and 3 lb. 2 oz. of salt goes into every 100 lb. of curd. This sort of Cheshire, more crumbly than a Cheddar and less pungent, has been by many put a fraction higher than a Stilton for flavour and eating excellence.

Another thing about Cheshire; it has not been copied so much as Cheddar (one inevitably compares the two) and it is said that this is because the soil does indeed play a great part in the production of the special flavour. At any rate you are *safer* with Cheshire. If you go into a grocer's shop for a piece of Stilton or Cheddar or Caerphilly, you have to poke, nibble, cross question and prod or you will find yourself with a piece of white chalk or a substance which takes the skin from your mouth. Cheshire is always excellent.

Blue Cheshire. At the moment no one tries to make Cheshire with blue veins in it. This could be done, one supposes, by needling and inoculating with a fungus. At the moment Cheshires turn blue through a lucky fault, about a month after manufacture if at all. There may be a manufacturer who deliberately "blues" Cheshire—but he would not advertise this because the sales talk in connection with them is that they are freaks.

Cotherstone. This cheese is also called Yorkshire Stilton. It is blue-veined and rarely seen. Before the war, about 1939, one could also get a white Cotherstone which tasted not unlike a cross between a Port Salut and a Bel Paese.

Derby. Quotes from

(1) *Grocer's Manual*—"Like Dunlop."

(2) O. Burdet, *Little Book of Cheese*—"Resembles Lancaster."

(3) *Complete Book of Cheese*—"A factory cheese said to be identical with Double Gloucester."

(4) U.S. Agriculture Handbook—"It is similar to Cheddar but it is not so firm and solid. . . ."

Which goes to show, doesn't it? I myself think that it is like a mild pale soapy Cheddar. See also **Sage Derby.**

Double Cottenham. Cottenham, population 2,440. Distance from Cambridge 6 miles, from London, 60. And an ugly little village, too. If you ask them there if they have ever heard of the cheese named after the place, they will gawp with surprise. However, in 1934 or thereabouts it did exist and a Cambridge firm called Messrs. Flack and Judge, Provision Merchants, used to send supplies up with regularity to London. At that time it was creamier and better than good Stilton. Very few references to it exist.

Dunlop. This cheese should have a separate heading under Scotland, for that is where it is made, mainly in the County of Ayr. It is Scotland's only national cheese. It is deep cream, more or less a copy of Cheddar.

Gloucester Double and Single. No confusion can exist worse than that which has come about from the pens of various writers describing—in the past 100 years—the difference between Single Gloucester cheese and Double Gloucester cheese. The muddle is not mainly the fault of the writers, because this cheese has had an odder caseous career than any other in Great Britain. This is what they say: *Hotel and Catering Review*, April 1956: ". . . two cheeses the Single and the Double Gloucester. The Single, a cream cheese, is not being made at present. Double Gloucester resembles its county neighbour the

Cheddar, but it is flatter in shape and matures more quickly, has a moister and runnier texture, with a mellow and fairly full flavour."

A famous *Grocery Manual*, Third Edition about 1934: "These cheeses are more solid in texture than Cheshire, less flaky and more waxy in consistency and more like Cheddar. The cheese has a clear yellow tint, with veins of blue mould and its flavour should be mild. It is made in two sizes, Single Gloucester or Berkeley, which is 2 or 3 inches thick and weighs about 14 lb., and Double Gloucester, double the thickness and weight. The terms 'Single' and 'Double' have only reference to the weight and not to quality. . . . The method of making is the same as that of Cheddars. When they have been in the ripening cellars for a month, the coat is coloured by being brushed over with beer containing Spanish brown or Indian red."

Agriculture Handbook, U.S. Department of Agriculture, (December 1953): "Gloucester and Derby are said to be almost identical and are made in practically the same way. Single Gloucesters, made originally in farm dairies, are 16 inches in diameter, between 2 and 3 inches thick and weigh about 15 lb. Double Gloucesters, which have become relatively uncommon, are also 16 inches in diameter, but they are between 4 and 5 inches thick and weigh about 24 lb. . . . The surface of an uncoloured cheese is clear yellow and is said to have well developed blue mould on the sides."

Farming for Pleasure and Profit (1879): "*Gloucester Cheese*— There are two kinds of cheese made in Gloucestershire— Single and Double Gloucester, but the mode of making either is the same except that the former is thinner, being called 'toasting cheese', and originally intended for that once favourite dish 'Welsh rarebit' is somewhat less salty and pressed for one day less in the course of its manufacture. It is occasionally also made somewhat less rich than the Double Gloucester by being partially mixed with skimmed milk."

A New History of Gloucestershire by Samuel Rudder (Ciren-cester, 1779): "In this Vale (of Gloucester) is made that fine cheese so deservedly esteemed not only in Great Britain but in all countries wherever it has been carried. The hundreds of Thornbury and the lower division of Gaumbaldy Ash, produce the best.

"It is made of various thicknesses from about ten pounds to a quarter of a hundredweight each. The thick sort is called Double Gloucestershire and Double Berkeley and usually sells on the spot at sixpence a pound. It requires to be kept to an age proportionate to its size and thickness to make it ready for the table."

The Rural Economy of Gloucestershire, including its Dairy, by William Marshall (1796): (This is the most accurate account of early English cheese-making that exists. Page upon page is taken up describing in the minutest detail the method of making and treating the curd in the two vales—those of Gloucester and Berkeley.) Here are some points from his work:

The colouring by anatto of the cheese he considers a crime and a deception, but he notes that in order to make buyers think that it contained much richness, it had long been practised.

In the cheese room the floor was prepared by rubbing it with beantops, potato haulm (he spells it halm, the older way) until it was a wet black colour. This was to make the blue coat rise. The cheeses were turned twice a week and the floor done fortnightly. This made the rinds tough as leather.

The Vale of Berkeley made better cheeses although this Vale also made the Single or thin shape. Locally the doubles were called Double Berkeley and not Double Gloucester and often the rinds were painted; a fake which he abominated, and which the dairymaids hated doing.

Mr. Marshall also pointed out that as the anatto colouring had spread to other counties and had then ceased to be a distinction, therefore the painting of the rind was done to make a new distinction.

What an extraordinary picture emerges. It's coloured yellow, painted red, rolled on a blue floor. It's supposed to have a blue mould on the outside yet there is no mention of blue veining. Single is the same as Double or smaller. Single is a poorer cheese and made with less creamy milk. It's like Derby: it's a cross between Cheddar and Cheshire.

Many little things have combined to create this stupendous confusion. In the first place so very little has been written on cheese that most writers have cribbed others where they have found references and the same mistake appears in several different books. Then the Gloucesters were rubbed with the potato haulm (as well as it being put on the floor of the cheese storing rooms) to (so the rubbers imagined) keep out cheese mites. This caused the blueness and this accounts for vague suggestions that it has a blue inside. But Samuel Rudder's "It requires to be kept to *an age proportionate to its size and thickness*, etc.", gives us the real answer to the greatest muddle. One tends to forget (it must be continuously stressed) that the longer, within reasonable bounds, a good and creamy cheese is kept the better it becomes.

Suppose suddenly that Stiltons were made in hoops or moulds of 7 instead of 14 lb., but the same way and using exactly the same quality milk. This smaller Stilton, maturing twice as fast as the larger, would taste at its point of perfection markedly less good. Furthermore, people knowing that it was a faster maturing size would tend to eat it before it was ripe. Suppose next that the larger Stilton was called a Double Stilton, it does not need much of a stretch of imagination to see how on being asked why it was so called, as each person explained to the next, the Double would have also stood for "doubly good" as well as the size. Then the smaller Stiltons would lose reputation so fast that the makers would get little for them and getting little for them, they would start to use more skimmed milk in the making.

That surely is the history of Double and Single Gloucester, with one more thing to add: note the large number of references to its excellence in the past; note how in 1955, in spite of a vigorous campaign to get British farmhouse cheeses on the go again, none appeared. The answer is that, in spite of its greatness, it has never been made and marketed consistently over a long period, another reason for the confusion and for the different other types it is said to resemble.

But here is the latest information of what it tastes and looks like. It is a large cartwheel affair, rather like a good mild Cheddar.

Lancashire. Here, for once, all references to this cheese in older works, are, so far as taste and texture are concerned, unanimous.

Lancashire is the best cheese for making Welsh Rarebit in the world. The reason is that it is far more crumbly than its cousins Cheshire and Cheddar and can even be spread on to bread or toast with a knife. When young it is mild and only slightly acid, but when it has finished maturing (three months it takes) it becomes mellow and even more flavoursome than Cheddar or Cheshire.

Actually, it gets its unique flavour, its softness and crumbliness from its rather unusual method of making.

It starts with the evening's milk cooled and placed in a cheese vat where it remains till the following morning. Then the morning's milk is added, the whole warmed to the renneting temperature. Then the curd is formed and next it is cut (as with nearly all cheeses) into tiny cubes.

The next stage in the process of making is that which accounts for the special qualities of Lancashire, for the fresh curd is mixed with old curd made the previous day and therefore having a greater acidity. Sometimes even three different days' curd is used.

The shape and size of the cheese vary. They used mainly to make great cartwheel ones of 40 to 50 lb. together with little 12 lb. affairs, 7 inches in diameter and 10 inches thick. These latter are now the more popular. The best Lancashire comes from the Fylde, that is the area north of the Ribble, bordering on the Irish Sea coast.

It doesn't come to the south of England nearly enough. When toasted, it has the consistency of a good hot custard—and a wonderful taste.

Leicester. This was once the second greatest cheese in England. It had a serious relapse before the last world war, but there are signs that it is on the way back again in popularity. Messrs. Tuxford and Tebbut (lovely name!), who also make meat pies, have a first-rate reputation for making farmhouse Leicestershires, and can sell all they can make.

These cheeses have the shape of a millstone and weigh some 40 lb. The texture is loose and flaky and rather more crumbly than a Cheshire, and the colour is a lightish red: it is anatto dye that does it.

Sage Derby. This was very good. The alternate layers of speckled green, which were the chopped sage which had been put in, made it extraordinarily appetising to the eye. Has it been seen since the war?

St. Ivel. This excellent cream cheese—when ripe—is an English version of a rather stiff Yoghurt.

"The milk used in the manufacture of St. Ivel Lactic cheese," it says on the label, "is scientifically treated with a pure culture of *Lactobacillus bulgaricus* (which has been called 'The Bacillus of Long Life') specially prepared by skilled Bacteriologists."

"The only cheese awarded a GOLD MEDAL
By the International Medical Congress, London."

"The culture in the cheese will remain active until . . . After this date, the cheese will continue to mature but the culture will become less active."

This last statement is interesting; in my opinion it is only near or actually after the culture activity date that this simple cream cheese begins to lose its humdrum flavour and becomes gastronomically interesting. Put a ripe St. Ivel on a cheese-board with some of the better cheeses of Europe, without its wrapping, and hint that it was flown over from the Continent—and it could become quite a vogue.

Slipcote or Slipcoat. Sometimes Stilton cheeses will burst their shape and spill down into a soft mass. They are taken away and eaten without waiting for them to ripen. Then they are called Slipcotes or Slipcoats. But more commonly, it stood for a very old cream cheese made in Rutland and Yorkshire, rarely seen in London, and when ripe not unlike Camembert. You would think by the name that it was a cheese which had slipped or fallen out of its coat. This probably is *not* correct. Slip is a very old English word (from the Norwegian probably, Slipa=slime) meaning (*a*) a soft semi-liquid mass, (*b*) curdled milk. Cote is an old word for a shed where things were made or stored. Salte-cote was the place where salt was made on the sea shore.

Stilton. All aboard the coach! Had you wanted to travel to Glasgow in the early part of the eighteenth century, you would have set off from Aldersgate Street in the City and then a while later (along what is now the A1 road) you would have stopped at the Bell, Stilton, to stretch legs, feed and generally revictual. At the end of the meal Landlord Cooper Thornhill would have offered you a cheese which, had you asked him the name, he would probably have called either Lady Beaumont's Cheese or Quenby, after a fine old Elizabethan Mansion some seven miles from Leicester. But when you got to Glasgow or wherever it was and were telling your friends of the superb creamy blue-veined wonder you had, you would have forgotten the name the landlord gave it, and called it "that cheese I had at Stilton".

This is not a conjecture; it is fact. No Stilton cheese was ever made at Stilton, but Landlord Cooper Thornhill married one of the daughters of Elizabeth Scarbow. One Christmas Mrs. Paulet who had married a farmer of that name of Wynoldham, sent her sister Mrs. Thornhill a cheese as a present which became so popular that the Bell Inn promised to take all that Mrs. Paulet could supply. Thus it was the two daughters of Elizabeth Scarbow carried on the good work.

Who first made Stilton? To give the Scarbow-Paulet family the palm would be to put the research worker on dangerous ground on account of two lines in Alexander Pope's *Imitation of Horace*:

> Cheese such as men in Suffolk make
> But wished it Stilton for his sake.

Now Pope would not have given a *new* name to a cheese unless he was fairly well satisfied that it would convey something to the minds of his readers. We can therefore say that Stilton was known even in London some time in George II's days, perhaps even as much as half a century before Mrs. Paulet made it.

Actually at some period between the two world wars there was quite a movement to erect a statue to Mrs. Paulet. After all, there is a statue to Madam Harel in France, the inventor of Camembert, so why not, they said? The scheme got as far as a Committee, with Sir John Squire at the head, but the scheme fell through.

Jane Austen also has a reference to Stilton cheese. In one

of the innumerable (how they all must have suffered from corns!) tedious walks which her chief characters have to take, she so contrives it that Mr. Elton gives his "fair companion an account of yesterday's party at Cole's, and that she was to come in herself for the Stilton cheese and the North Wiltshire, the butter, the celery, the beetroot and all the dessert".

And Charles Lamb writing to Thomas Allsop in 1823 pays Stella a pretty compliment. "Your cheese is the best I have ever tasted. Mary has sense enough to value the present; for she is very fond of Stilton. Yours is the delicatest, rainbow-hued, melting piece I have ever tasted."

★　　　★　　　★

How is this blue-veined wonder made? Let us journey up to Webster's dairy, one of a number of homes of real farmhouse Stilton at Saxilby, near Melton Mowbray, and see all.

Farmer T. R. Stockdale will be there to welcome you as was his grandfather before him and as will his son when he retires. It is a true family business with a tradition.

First in goes the milk into a great stainless steel vat. It takes 400 gallons and in shape it is oblong, low and of the same proportions as an ordinary bath, like one for a medium-sized giant.

After the warming, renneting and curd-cutting (for all of which see Chapter Two), the curd is ladled out into straining cloths and these are placed over the curd sink for the whey to run out into a cistern to feed pigs. At Webster's dairy they have been even more labour-saving than this, for the whey runs out through pipes under the public road which runs through Saxilby to the piggery opposite the dairy.

After a while and when sufficient whey has drained off, a lot of salt is added and the curd is then put into hoops, that is cylindrical casings open at each end which used to be made of wood and now are made of steel. They are 8 inches in diameter and 10 or more inches deep. In the side of the hoops are small holes less than the diameter of a farthing for the purpose of further whey draining.

On the first day they may be turned several times. From the

second to the sixth, seventh or eighth days they will be turned once.

After this they come out of their hoop homes and they are scraped and smoothed over with a knife. Next the young Stilton is wrapped in a linen cloth. Those who have watched a mother or nurse wrap up a newly born baby in a napkin will have noticed the deft way in which the pin goes in and out of the cloth without scratching the child. The way in which the dairy-maid whips the coarse white linen round the young cheese (26 gallons of milk make 1 Stilton of 15 lb.—1 gallon milk produces 1 lb. curd, but half of this with Stilton evaporates), and then drives in the murderous looking steel pins, is most evocative of the other operation.

After this the cheeses may, but more often don't, go back into the hoops. Then they go into another room where they stay, still being turned until the rind is sufficiently strong to withstand the bindings coming away. This process lasts anything from a week to fourteen days and this is the time they are in the "coating" room.

The next stage on the journey is to the maturing room. Here it is that the blue veins form; here, too, a comment of some importance: none of the very few books on cheese give satisfactory explanations as to how the blue veins get there. Either the authors don't quite know or possibly they feel that (just as wine writers gloss over all mention of the great use of sulphur in wine-making) an explanation takes away the glamour. Maybe the method has changed in the last half-century.

In the early years of this century, Rider Haggard published a book *Rural England* and in it described the recipe for making Stilton. It is simple, lucid and obviously very accurate. Here is how it ends: "It is then moved into a coating room (which must be kept damp and have a cool draught of air passing through it where it remains for a week or more) and the surface assumes its light grey colour. After this it is transferred to the store room where it is turned and brushed for a period of six months. Now if all things have gone right it should be a perfect Stilton, etc., etc.", with never a word about how the veins or mould come.

Next an American Agricultural Handbook got out by the U.S.

Department of Agriculture: "The mould said to be *Penicillium Roqueforti* gradually develops in the curd."

In a recent food book, Messrs. Aplin and Barrett Limited, in a letter explaining about bacteria, make the following statement regarding Stilton:

"The green mould cheese such as Stilton is of course particularly dependent upon the action of the mould *Penicillium Roqueforti* for the special flavour. It is not normally necessary to add the mould artificially in premises where the cheese is regularly made, since the buildings themselves become more or less permanently infected.

"When Stilton cheese is made in a new location, however, it is a great advantage to add a culture of the mould during the first few weeks of manufacture. We ourselves decided to manufacture Stilton cheese in Somerset and were told that it would be quite impossible to do so outside the Stilton district of Leicestershire. We adopted, however, the expedient of artificially adding a suitable mould culture at first and were completely successful in making first-grade Stilton."

Lastly from *Farming For Pleasure and Profit* by Arthur Roland (Chapman and Hall, 1879):

"Nearly two years is required to bring Stilton cheeses to perfect maturity, which are not generally considered at their best until somewhat decayed. The blue mould may be communicated from an old cheese to a much younger one by removing pieces of the former with the cheese scoop or taster and interchanging them. The operation in fact consists of the transposition of the mould plant from one to the other which grows in most damp warm cellars, but the cheeses selected for the inoculation should, however, of themselves be dry and the blue mould of the old cheese be quite free from any portion bearing a more decayed aspect."

Now all these statements may be and probably are accurate, but they don't describe what is common practice in the Stilton-making area today. What happens at Webster's dairy is this: each young cheese is pierced horizontally sixty times on three different occasions (i.e. 180 stabs in all) with a stainless steel affair which looks like a thinnish knitting needle attached to a wooden handle. And there is sufficient of the mould in the air for this operation to be sufficient to start the veining.

The practice is universal, and at a large establishment near by, where the cheese is made on a co-operative basis, the same thing is done semi-mechanically, for the cheeses are put on to a little rotating platform, a foot lever is pressed down and the cheese is pierced by a dozen stabs, six on each side; so the sixty piercings are done with only five lever pressings.

After this the Stilton continues to ripen until it reaches your table around three to six months from the day it was milk. But it is not always easy to stop the flow of milk and in the summer months people don't feel like Stilton and anyway the milk is not so good, so that is when white Stilton is made. It is quite good, but it doesn't get the piercing and isn't matured.

Cutting and Serving. You have probably thought until now that the finest way, the most correct way, the most gastronomic way to serve a Stilton was to cut it in half and wrap half round with a fine lawn napkin and then to dig into the centre with an ivory handled silver cheese scoop. Furthermore, you have been brought up to believe that if you want your Stilton to taste even better than best, you pour into it a large noggin of good port. Both these theories have long been questioned by those who took the art of eating seriously, but by and large both practices were held to be sound. Now, however, the Stilton Manufacturers' Association have pronounced against both and what they say is reasonable:

"It is widely assumed," says their pamphlet, "that the correct method of serving Stilton is with a spoon from half a cheese and that port wine poured into it improves the flavour. Both these assumptions are false. The use of the spoon causes a large amount of waste and as for the port, if the cheese is good it requires no port, whilst if it is not good, no amount of port will improve it, though of course Stilton cheese and port wine go well together."

Note the little sales talk at the end. But it is true that these two, like Leicester cheese and watercress, are bound together by a knot more eternal than a marriage bond.

America has discovered this, by the way, and there is marketed on the other side of the Atlantic a mixture of port wine and Stilton cheese in a tube with a screw cap. "A gentle squeeze and with all the smooth controlled facility of toothpaste consigning it-self to the brush, a distillation of the pastures of Leicestershire Vale of Belvoir and an essence of the sunny alien vineyards of Spain (sic) is delivered in a gastronomic alliance."

Actually as regards the pouring of port into the cheese, the pamphlet of the Stilton Manufacturers doesn't state the case quite comprehensively enough and we have in T. G. W. Wiles of Long Clawson an acknowledged expert of the district who agrees with me in the following more accurate statement: "A fair drenching of port will mask the faults of an imperfect grade, but there is not a vintage in the world that will improve a good one."

Cutting. The Stilton makers have again only got half the story and have also been a little too terse. The way they recommend it being cut is that the whole cheese should be cut in half and then that slices should be made flatwise across the face.

The advantage of this way is not only that it is far less waste-ful but that no portion of the cheese is exposed for any length of time to the air without being cut. In other words it always stays moist.

In other words, it all boils down to: Are you going to eat it slowly? If so, slice. Or quickly? Then get the extra aesthetic pleasure of the silver scoop. The actual flavour is identical either way.

Storing. I quote the Stilton cheese-makers verbatim, for their advice is excellent. "Keep the cheese at room temperature covered with a cloth. Cheese which has been allowed to go dry should be covered with a cloth which has been damped with brine (a handful of common salt in a basin of water). The recovery of texture and flavour will be assisted by a little warmth. A fluctuating temperature will ruin a good cheese. The optimum temperature is approximately 58° F."

And that is about all on what Daniel Defoe in his *Tour Through England and Wales* (1724) called "this magnificent cheese" when he took some at the Bell Inn at Stilton.

Swaledale. A soft white cheese made in Yorkshire. Swale is from the old Norse meaning a low lying place, somewhere cool.

Wensleydale. From the ancient, rambling and attractive

town of Wensleydale in the valley of the River Ure, Yorkshire. Here is the home (though the cheese is made in all the valleys around) of what some call the rival and others say is better than Stilton.

Wensleydale is of the same shape as Stilton, only often a little smaller and the rind instead of having a sort of mottled crinkly appearance, looks corrugated: this is because of the way the cloth is bound around the young cheese. Some say that blue veined (there is also a white which is excellent and popular) Wensleydale is a little more tangy than Stilton, others that it is more creamy. We say that they are very similar.

York Cream. Another name for Cambridge.

GREECE

Feta. The national cheese of Greece. It is a so-called "pickled cheese" made originally by shepherds in the mountainous region above Athens, and again originally of ewe's milk. It is a soft cheese and spicy.

Kasseri. A hard cheese made from ewe's milk.

Mitzithra. Also called Pot Cheese. This is a by-product of the famous Feta in so much as the whey left over from this latter is added to fresh milk and the two are curdled.

Kopanisti. This is a blue cheese.

Kefalotyi. This is Greek for hat because this is the shape of the cheese. A hard grating cheese made of goat's milk.

Teleme. A very quickly ripening cheese made all over Greece, Turkey and Bulgaria. Like Feta.

HOLLAND

The Dutch cheese-lover is apt to remark about the number of varieties made in France, that while they have 200 (or so claim) different cheeses they are all of one flavour, whereas Holland has only two cheeses, yet each has 200 different nuances of taste.

It is the wives who make the cheese in this country and the pride they take in 'it is wonderful. When Sundays come round and neighbours drop in for a morning coffee, it is the cheese room which is thrown open to inspection and sampling, just as is the wine cellar in Burgundy.

Edam. Was first made around Edam in North Holland. It is also called Tête de Moine and Katzen-Kopf. It is all factory made, there is no farmhouse Edam. The fat content is never high and it is copied by every cheese-making country in the world. The shape is that of a flattened football and when exported the cheeses are coloured bright red and then rubbed with wax. The taste is of pleasant soap. Usual weight: 3 to 4 lb.

Gouda. This cheese can be either farmhouse or factory and was first made around Gouda in South Holland. Cheese-making in the Netherlands is a big industry and it is quite a thought that highly trained young men working with elaborate machines and perfect premises can never turn out a factory Gouda to touch the quality of a farmhouse one.

This cheese much resembles the Edam, but it contains more fat. A farmhouse Gouda will keep and mature and will eventually become worthy of the table, for it becomes strong without bite. These cheeses are fairly hard in texture, are shaped like a football but not coloured red. Weight about 12 lb.

Leyden. There is Leyden and Old Leyden, named after the university town of that name. Both are cheeses with caraway seeds in them, but the old Leyden is well matured and the seeds have imparted a pretty good kick. Little is exported.

Fruidhagel. Not only is none of this cheese exported, but little sees its way even to the Hague. It is a Friesian product made with Friesian cow's milk and is impregnated with cloves. The flavour is delightful, but when the cheeses mature, they become extremely strong.

HUNGARY

Liptauer. This is named after the province of Liptow in the north of Hungary and is normally white. It would be interesting to find out how and when it emigrated (especially to Austria) and became the excellent red coloured mix-up we now know.

Ingredients: 4 oz. cream cheese, 4 oz. butter, 1 oz. chopped capers, 5 chopped anchovies, 1 small teaspoon of french mustard, 1½ teaspoons ground paprika.

Mix all together and put into a mould till ready to serve.

Other variations are to change the capers for very finely chopped black olives; and yet another is to put in chopped tinned red pimentos.

INDIA

In India, Burma, Ceylon, Pakistan and most Oriental countries, cheese as we understand it is almost unknown. The reason is that it is all consumed as Yoghurt.

Surati. India's best known cheese. It is named after the town of Surat (Bombay State) and is a cottage cheese variety.

The curd is held in very small bamboo baskets the size of a breakfast cup, and the whey is drained out of the bamboo strips and is churned twice. Weight 3 to 4 oz.

IRELAND

This country has no traditional cheeses or if they did have they have been forgotten. Now under the Department of Agriculture a few factory Cheddars are turned out, together with processed cheese.

ITALY

We are apt to think of Gorgonzola as the prime cheese of Italy, followed by Bel Paese; actually the one which is of even greater importance is Parmesan, and yet this name is not often used for this type of cheese in Italy itself.

As far back as A.D. 1200 a group of Italian cheeses have been made which are referred to as Grana. The first characteristic is that they are granular in body texture and taste—hence the name. They have an exquisite taste, are very hard and thus suitable for grating, have splendid keeping qualities even in hot weather and (a great help for the export business) require little special packing. When young—that is under a year old—such cheese is excellent for table purposes as well. As we list hereunder the names of Italian cheeses, we shall indicate which are Grana type.

Asiago. This is a grana-type cheese semi-cooked. It is round and flat weighing around 20 lb. and originated from a commune of the same name in the province of Vicenza. It resembles Peccorino Romano.

Bel Paese. This is Italian for "beautiful country" and is not a generic name, but a trade name. It is a newcomer to Italy, not having been marketed much before 1921. It was first made in Melzo, Upper Lombardy. You will also find Bel Paese sold under the following names: Fior d'Alpe, Savoia, Caccio, Reale (royal cheese) and Vittoria.

In flavour this is one of the mildest cheeses in existence. It is classed as soft rather than semi-soft, though it never runs like Brie, Camembert or Pont l'Evêque. In colour it is pearly white. Texture rubbery in the pleasantest way imaginable.

Fresh whole cow's milk is used, preferably pasteurised. It is "started" with an active lactic acid to the strength of 0·25 per cent. when the temperature should be about 108° F. Rennet is added to see that the curd sets in 20 minutes, often less.

Then the curd is cut, first by hand, then with a rake to prevent it matting and to get the whey out quickly. Then the curd is transferred to moulds. From the time the lactic acid is added to the time the embryo cheese is put into moulds only 30 minutes elapses.

After they have been turned for a while the cheeses are given a bath for nearly a day in an 18 per cent. brine solution at a temperature of 55° F. Then they go to a curing room where the temperature is 40° F., and a little fine salt is sprinkled on the cheese.

After this, once the curing starts a brownish slime appears on the skin. This is desirable and helps give the finished cheese its characteristic flavour. Weight 4½ lb., 6 inches in diameter. A Bel Paese is ready for the table within five weeks of making.

Bitto. Similar to Fontina and was first made in Friuli (also called Friaul) and also in the Adda Valley.

Bra. Named after a village in Piedmont where it was first made by nomads. It is salty, hard and white and weighs about 12 lb. per cheese.

Buttiro. This is a Calabrian version of a Caciocavallo, only a large knob of butter is placed inside the cheese (which is shaped like a giant elongated fir cone), so that when it is cut one gets—

like slicing a hard boiled egg—a piece of butter and cheese from the same segment.

Caciocavallo. No, this cheese is not made from mare's milk as some imagine, but has got its name from the fact that two cheeses (they usually weigh 4 to 6 lb.) are often tied together by string and so look as if astride a horse. This cheese has a delicate flavour, an exceptionally smooth firm texture and is quite white. It tastes like a cross between a Gruyère and a Cheddar.

Crescenza. Often called Stracchino Crescenza. Made in Lombardy from September to April. Weight anything from 1 to 3 lb.

Fontina. One of the fullest cheeses of Italy, somewhat yellow, between semi-soft and hard, made from ewe's milk in the Aosta Valley in Piedmont. It is made in the same way as a Gruyère and often has a few small round eyes.

Gorgonzola. When French gastronomes aver that this lovely truly creamy yet strong blue-veined cheese is merely a copy of Roquefort, they speak like fools. Gorgonzola is not meant to be a copy and never was, for its uniqueness is its creaminess as we have said, whereas the French ewe's milk cheese is crumbly, friable and very salty.

Gorgonzola gets its name from a village not far from Milan, though rather like our Welsh Caerphilly, hardly any is made there now, the industry being confined to the province of Lombardy. The name of the mould used to give it its blue veins is *Penicillium Glaucum* (it is also called *Penicillium Roqueforti*); it is sprinkled as a mould powder alternatively on evening and morning curd and the cheeses then put into wooden hoops lined with cloth. The distribution of the curd is important, and roughly speaking, the evening curd goes in the centre, leaving the morning for the outside. Maturing time always more than ninety days, often six months and even a year. Weight: 14 to 17 lb.

Incanestrato. This is a very popular Italian cheese, similar to or really the same as Pecorino, except that it is pressed in wicker moulds and one often sees the imprint of the wicker on the sides of the cheese. *Incanestrato* means basketed.

Often pepper is added and then it is called Incanestrato pepato.

Majocchino. This is a cheese similar to Incanestrato only made in the province of Messina in Sicily, and with the addition of olive oil.

Mascarpone. A very soft, fresh, cream cheese made in Lombardy only during the winter. It is sold in little muslin bags and only weighs 4 oz. each cheese. It is eaten with fruit and sprinkled with cinnamon. Like Picotta, it is occasionally smoked by the peasants. It is sometimes made with the addition of lemon juice.

Montasio. Very similar to Bitto and made in the same region. Weight between 25 and 35 lb., and cured for as long often as two years. Often the rind is blackened with soot.

Mozzarella. If there were more buffaloes in Italy, there would be more Mozzarella cheese. You can eat it either very fresh like a Scamorze or matured like a Caciocavallo, both of which it resembles. Weight about 12 oz.

Pannarone. Also called white Gorgonzola, this is a cheese made in Lower Lombardy with a slightly bitter-sweet taste. It is of course without the blue veins. Weight between 17 and 22 lb.

Parmesan. The Italians take the maturing of a good Grana cheese as seriously as does the French peasant his wine. There are several types of Parmesan made in Italy, but the inhabitants of Parma in the province of Emilia claim theirs to be the best. Parma cheese in England is called Parmesan; in Parma, it is called **Parmigiano,** and the older it is the better and more costly it is. Vecchio (old) is the two-year matured, Stravecchio (extra old) three years and Stravecchione (quite old) the four years. After some six months, it is given the coating which gives the cheese its characteristic appearance, and which consists of a mixture of lamp-black and burnt umber mixed in wine.

The quality of these cheeses is tested by experts who tap the outside with special little hammers and predict how they will turn out.

Pecorino. There are several types of Pecorino, but that which takes first place is Pecorino Romano, a hard cheese made with ewe's milk. It is a grating cheese and much liked by those who want something rather aromatic. When this same cheese is made from cow's milk, it is called Vacchino Romano and when from goat's milk, Caprino Romano. When only cured for five to eight months, it is used as a table cheese, when longer, for grating.

Provolone. This cheese is a very close relation to Caciocavallo but contains more fat and is smoked before it is salted and dried. It makes a better table cheese than Caciocavallo, especially when it has been cured for around eight months.

Ricotta. Let us get one thing right about Ricotta, Scamorze, Mozzarella, Broccio, Ziger and other similar cheeses; it is also called albumen cheese and this means that, due to the way it is cooked (often live steam is injected into the whey) the albumen rises to the surface and then goes into cheese cloths. Now the point is that you can consume it at once, in which case it is like a cottage cream cheese, or you can have it "dry", in which case it is suitable for grating like a Parmesan.

Robbiola. Similar to Crescenza. Circular and flat. Weight from 8 oz. to 2 lb.

Robbiolini. Almost the same as Robbiola, only each individual cheese weighs about $3\frac{1}{2}$ oz.

Sardo. When Pecorino Romano is made on the island of Sardinia, it is called Sardo. Formerly, it was made solely of ewe's milk, now it is done with cow's and ewe's mixed.

Scamorze. First made in Abruzzi in central Italy from buffalo's milk, now it has become so popular that its production has spread all over and it is also made with cow's and goat's milk. Size that of a large turkey's egg.

Stracchino. This is a generic name, given to a type of uncooked very creamy sort of cheese rather like a Bel Paese but ripened only for some ten to fourteen days.

Taleggio. Named after the Taleggio Valley in the Province of Lombardy and a comparative newcomer to Italian cheeses since it was not created until after the 1914-1918 War. It is a Stracchino variety, made of whole milk, quite soft and square. Weight 3 to 4 lb.

Veneto. Also called Venezza. One of the Parmesan type cheeses. It is very similar to Asiago.

JAPAN

An inquiry to the Japanese Embassy whether they had any national cheeses brought by return air mail samples of Japanese copies of traditional European cheeses. These were all called "Snow Brand" and were excellent copies, superbly packaged.

Japan started research in 1915 and in 1925 began "to make cheese for sale in markets". My informant does not say which markets, but adds that in 1955 Japan produced 2,698,621 lb. of cheese.

MEXICO

Asadero. Also called **Oaxaca.** This is a white whole milk cheese which has the peculiarity of quickly melting when cooked. Asadero means "suitable for roasting".

Anejo. Sometimes this is covered with ground chili powder and then called Enchilado. What heat!

NEW ZEALAND

This country possesses no cheeses of her own creation. New Zealand Cheddar represents 99 per cent. of the cheese made. A copy of Danish Blue has been successfully carried out; production most limited.

NORWAY

Gjetost. The *gjet* means goat and the *ost* means cheese. There is more in it than that, though. This has been the national cheese of Norway for over 100 years and now it is usually made with cow's milk to the extent of 90 per cent. and goat 10 per cent. Whether the latter is to give it an added flavour or whether it is done so that the goat part of the word should have some semblance of truth, is not clear.

Before describing Gjetost, I ask you to believe that the flavour does not deserve the cruel epithets which have been hurled at it. It has been likened to bad toffee, mouldy hay, sweet manure, patent medicine, and also to tobacco, but is like none of these. It *is*, though, utterly different from our conception of cheese, and as such it is an acquired taste, and when acquired delicious.

The process is to boil the whey and cream in huge stainless steel vats, until they are reduced to about a quarter of their original volume. Stirring must take place all the time, the better to expel the water. Sugar is added and the result is exactly like a sweet-sour (the sugar taste is predominant and pleasant) fudge. It is marketed in small square blocks and wrapped in thick waxed paper. It keeps indefinitely and its nourishment value is immense. I think it delicious with butter and digestive biscuits.

Gammelost. This is Norwegian for old cheese. A really potent cheese made from sour skim-milk mainly, in the counties of Hardanger and Sogu.

During the making it undergoes every thrashing and boiling conceivable until it ends up by being packed in straw that has been impregnated with juniper extract.

Fløtost. Fløte in Norwegian means cream. It is similar to the famous Mysost save that it contains more cream.

Mysost. You can call this the national cheese not only of Norway, but of all the Scandinavian countries. It is the same in principle as Gjetost, save that it is made entirely of cow's milk whey. As with the other, the liquid is boiled for over five hours, being continuously stirred the while. When this is finished the albumens rise to the surface and are skimmed off. Then as much as 10 per cent. brown sugar is added and some manufacturers throw in cloves as well. In spite of this, it is still a good cheese.

Nøkkelost. A cheese frequently seen in London; rather like a Dutch Gouda with caraway seeds in it. Excellent when young; a bit strong for English taste when old. Inexpensive.

PORTUGAL

Saloio. Made near Lisbon from cow's skim-milk. A sort of tiny, strong-smelling, hard, moulded, peasant affair.

Serra de Estrella. Called after a mountain range of the same name considered the best place for cheese-making, this is the best type of cheese in Portugal. Usually it is made from all ewe's milk or occasionally from a mixture of ewe's and goat's milk. Flavour sharp and rather acid.

Rabacal. Made near Coimbra, the university town. A fairly firm cheese, flat and cylindrical and 5 inches across and of ewe's or goat's milk.

SPAIN

Cabrales. A goat's milk cheese made round Santander in North Spain. Not very good, at least they vary so much in quality that trying them out is a risky and dull task. They are blue-veined cheeses.

Manchego. Made in the dry central plateau of La Mancha and from a breed of sheep called by the same name. That is how the cheese gets its name. Butter fat content very high, production very uneven in quality as it is made by peasants.

Roncal. A hard cheese, made to keep and to be used for grating. This is one of Spain's few cow's milk cheeses and gets its name from the Roncal Valley up in the province of Navarre.

Villalon. Like Manchego this is ewe's milk cheese, made in central Spain mainly in the province of Valladolid. The cheeses are in the shape of small, long, round cylinders, are soft and eaten as soon as made.

SWEDEN

Herrgårdost. This is a close copy of a rather hard Emmental. It is also called Manor Cheese and is perhaps Sweden's most popular cheese. Weight around 26 to 40 lb. per cheese. Aroma excellent.

Prestost (Priest Cheese). Made in Sweden for 200 years. A hard cheese of which the rind is washed with whisky the first three days of maturing. Sweden also copies quite well Stilton, Roquefort, Gorgonzola, Camembert and Port Salut.

Steppe. This cheese was originally made in Russia. It is a hard cheese with round gas holes, like a cross between a Dutch Gouda and a Swiss Emmental.

Sueciaost. Some spell it Sveciaost, but whichever way you do, all it means is Swedish cheese. Actually, it is a moderate copy of a Gouda, but there are many variations up and down the country. Nearly always Sveciaost is of open texture. Open is the best translation of the Swedish word *grynpipig*, a term used to describe small mechanical holes and not "gas holes". Sweden eats about twice as much of this cheese as she does of all her other varieties put together. They also do a spiced Suecia with caraway seeds and cloves.

Vastgota. Made in the province of Vastergotland. A hard cheese rather like a Svecia or Emmental.

SWITZERLAND

The Swiss manufacture French Government cigarettes under licence in Switzerland. Needless to say they are far better filled and more neatly wrapped than in France, for whatever she does Switzerland does well.

Swiss cheese-making, however, isn't just left to chance and the individual maker's honesty; the whole industry is controlled by the Federal Cheese Factory and Stable Inspectorate of which there are no less than 130 travelling inspectors.

Appenzell. Gets its name from the East Swiss Canton of Appenzell. It is made in a similar way to Emmental, but in Switzerland (it is not much exported) it is steeped in a liquor of cyder or white wine to which spices have been added.

Appenzell Rass. The same as the above only made with skim-milk and the soaking in the liquor goes on for several weeks. The resultant article is one of considerable pungency.

Bellelay. This cheese is also called Tête de Moine or Monks Head and was originally only made in the fifteenth century by the monks of the Abbey of Bellelay near Moutiers in the canton of Berne. This cheese has a soft buttery consistency and is over 50 per cent. fat. It takes over a year to mature, and will keep for four years in a cold cellar.

Weight 10 to 13 lb.—round, 6 to 8 inches in diameter.

Emmentaler. Gets its name from the Emmental Valley in the canton of Berne and has been known as a fine cheese from the sixteenth century.

It is a very hard cheese to make; three different types of bacteria are used as starters, *Propionibacterium stermanii* being the one which is responsible for the eyes forming.

According to regulations, an Emmental for export must weigh not less than 145 lb. (but these great millstones are usually nearer 160 lb. in weight) and the fat content must be 45 per cent. minimum.

Method of Making. First never less than 2,000 lb. of milk

(2,500 lb. makes a cheese of 185 to 200 lb.) is put into a double-jacketed copper kettle which has a steam chamber at the bottom and is heated to some 86° F. After this, when the curd is firm enough to cut, a remarkable instrument known as a Swiss harp (it is like a very large tennis racquet with the string running only lengthwise) cuts the curd lengthwise into long rectangular strips of 1 inch thick. Five minutes later the curd is "harped" again; that is cut and mixed until the particles are some $\frac{1}{8}$ inch in diameter. Next the curd is "foreworked", that is stirred for half an hour, and when firm enough, it is heated to a temperature of 125° F. At this moment the Emmental to be looks like a bubbling mass of boiling breadcrumbs being agitated by a giant electric whisk. Remember that the boiling pan is 2 yards in diameter and is a yard high.

Now comes the moment to take the cheese out of the kettle or cauldron. It is scooped up into a coarsely woven dipping cloth which is attached to a sort of thick brass rail with a handle. This rail fits snugly round the cauldron enabling the cheese to be successfully scooped up into the cloth which hangs for a while above the cauldron and so the remaining whey drips away (sorry!).

Then the cheeses are pressed, put into a cold room (temperature 55° F.) and salted in brine. Ten days later they go into another warmer (65° F. to 70° F.) room for six weeks when the main maturing takes place, and it is here that the propionic acid starts making the holes. Finally the Emmental goes into a colder room for a further three or four months which can, at the request of customers wanting an extra fine cheese, be extended to a year.

Gruyère. Has been made in Switzerland for over 200 years, and is named after the valley of the same name in the canton of Fribourg. Now it is also made in the cantons of Vaud and Neuchâtel and the production is about a third that of Emmental. Its manufacture is very similar to that of this latter cheese. Here are the more important differences.

(1) A Gruyère weighs on an average only 80 lb.

(2) The curd is cut into larger pieces and is given a little more heat.

(3) The holes are smaller and less frequent.

(4) It is more heavily salted.

(5) The cheese takes longer to mature.

(6) The rind is more greasy than the Emmentaler and this means that an additional maturing takes place from the outside inwards.

(7) The fat content is higher at 48 per cent.

(8) The temperature of the curing cellar is distinctly lower and it is this which makes for the smaller eyes.

The taste is firm, almost hard, slightly acidulous. More creamy than Emmental.

Piora. This cheese is made in the Swiss Alps in the canton of Ticino and is either made of cow's milk or of a mixture of cow's and goat's milk. Tipo Piora and Vero Piora are the two varieties made from the former, while Uso Piora is made from the mixture. It has small eyes and is similar to Tilsiter. They are flat and round and weigh around 26 lb.

Saanen. Made in the Saanen Valley of the Bernese Oberland, it is also known as Hobelkäse (plane cheese) because it eventually becomes so hard that (in its district of origin) a special cheese plane has to be used to cut it.

The average maturing time for a Saanen is five years. Some times a cheese (they are similar to Emmental only the curd is heated at a very high temperature) will be "laid down", as the English do a pipe of port, at a child's birth and eaten at all anniversaries and feast days and finished at his burial. One such cheese was kept for 200 years.

Sbrinz. One of the oldest hard cheeses of Europe; the *caseus helveticus* mentioned by Columella was probably a Sbrinz, which gets its name from the town of Brienz in the Bernese Oberland. The production is less than a fifth that of Gruyère which it resembles, but

(1) it takes three years to cure and in consequence is very hard and so suitable for grating.

(2) The fat content is higher, nearly 50 per cent.

(3) The holes are either absent or only the size of a pin head.

(4) The dealer stores the cheese vertically not horizontally, and after a year the rind is rubbed over with linseed oil to prevent further evaporation and loss of weight.

Schabziger. Called also Green Cheese, Glarnerkäse and in America Sapsago. The word Schabziger comes from the German word *schaben* to grate, and *Ziger* a kind of cheese, and the Americans have got their word from this. In its present form the cheese has remained the same for five centuries.

This cheese is made from slightly sour skim-milk heated to boiling temperature. Then cold butter-milk is added. The task now is to precipitate the casein (the albuminous matter which is the chief constitution of all cheese) and this is done by stirring in sour whey. This is an important moment in the manufacture of Schabziger, for if too much whey goes in, the curd will be too soft; if too little it will be too hard.

When the cheese is made it has mixed into it the dried powdered leaves of blue melilot (*mililotus coerulea*) a sweet smelling kind of clover which the Greeks used to call honey lotus. This gives it an aromatically pungent flavour and makes it an excellent ingredient to grate with plenty of butter on to bread for sandwiches. The final shape is that of a flat-topped cone.

Spalen. This cheese gets its name from the wooden containers (*spalen*) in which they are shipped abroad and were first made in the canton of Unterwalden. They are in every way similar to Sbrinz, save that the Spalen are a younger, less mature variety and may not by law be sold as Sbrinz.

Toggenburger. Also called Bloder cheese, this is made in the Alps of St. Gall, in Toggenburg and in the Werdenberg district. It is also made in the Principality of Liechtenstein. It is Switzerland's only sour-milk cheese. It is made of skim-milk and takes six to nine months to cure. It does not form a rind but what is called a "Speckschicht" or a layer of fat. This cheese hardly ever leaves the district, being consumed by the farmers whose income comes from the butter they make.

Vacherin. This is a curious cheese; wonderful in taste when ripe, but only made (in Switzerland at least) in the autumn and in a dozen or so mountain dairies in the Joux Valley of the Vaud Canton. It is a very soft creamy white cheese, almost like a runny Brie, but within a very hard rind. Often it is eaten with a spoon. They take two or three months to mature, are from 6 to 11 lb. in weight, 8 inches to 12 inches in diameter and 2 inches to 3 inches in height. The marketing period ends with the warm weather, so the summer tourist seldom sees this fine cheese, but it makes a great treat for the winter skier.

Valais Raclette. Made only in the canton of Valais, this is used mainly for a special hot toasted dish called Raclette (see Chapter IV). The cheese weighs about 20 lb.

TURKEY

Most milk in Turkey is turned into yoghurt of which there are two grades. *Siliuri* has plenty of cream in it and is rated the better. Then comes *Yagsiz* made of skim-milk. Mostly yoghurt made with ewe's milk, but it doesn't matter what milk is used really.

Modern Turkey is very keen on her modern creameries, which go by the name of Mandira, where they make many European copies, including Roquefort.

Edirne. A soft white cheese made of ewe's milk with a fair proportion of butter fat, named after an important town near the Greek frontier.

Kaser. A medium hard cheese made originally in the extreme east of Turkey and usually of ewe's milk.

Kelle Peyniri. The Turkish word for cheese is *peyniri*. This particular one is almost extinct.

Mihalic. A soft cheese rarely seen.

VENEZUELA

Queso de Cincho. A fresh milk cheese eaten young.

YUGOSLAVIA

Sir is Serbo-croat for cheese and the root or origin is probably Indo-European.

Kajmak. Kajmak is a Turkish word meaning "cream."

Paski Sir. This comes from the island of Pag (Payo in Italian) and is made of sheep's milk and is sold in units of 2 to 10 lb. In taste and texture it is not far from an Italian Parmesan.

Sir Izmiješane. Izmiješati means "to mix."

Sir Masni. Masni means "fat".

Sir Posni. Posni means "meagre".

Trappist. This is another of those cheeses which have spread far beyond their original boundaries. It is most similar to French Port Salut and the great Canadian Oka and was first made in 1885 in a monastery near Banjalaka in Bosnia. Though semi-soft, it is cured like a hard cheese and ripens all through rather than only on the surface. In weight they vary from ones of 3 lb. and 5 lb. to over 10 lb.

Travnik. Also called Arnautski Sir. A soft whole milk cheese with a little goat's milk thrown in.

Appendix I

ADDITIONAL CHEESE VARIETIES

AMERICA

Camosun. The method of making this semi-soft, open-textured cheese was developed by Washington State College in order to use up surplus milk on farms. It takes less time than the granular or stirred-curd process. Drained curd is pressed in hoops about 6 in. in diameter and 7 in. deep, salted in brine for 30 hours, then coated with non-odorous paraffin wax and cured for 1 to 3 months in a humid room at 50–60°F.

FRANCE

Bougon. A popular goat's milk Poitou cheese very similar to Chabichou.

Niolo. A square, round-edged goat's milk cheese tasting most strongly of goat and made in Corsica.

Pelardou. One of the best goat's milk cheeses, possessing fragrance and delicacy of flavor. They are made exclusively in the mountains, are usually cylindrical in shape, but as each farmer is an individualist and has his own established routine, they may vary in shape.

Poivre d'Ane. Made in countryside farms in Upper Provence. It is moulded by hand into small flattened balls and packed with sprigs of rosemary and savory which impart a distinctive and pleasing flavour. Weight varies from 5–7 oz.

Providence. A cheese almost the same as Port du Salut made in the Département of Seine-et-Oise. Six inches in diameter, $2\frac{1}{2}$ in. thick and weight about $2\frac{1}{2}$ lb.

Thenay. Thenay, a soft, whole-milk cheese, resembles Camembert. It is made, and the larger part eaten, in the region of Thenay in the Département of Loir-et-Cher. Rennet is added to a mixture of evening and morning milk at a temperature of about 85°F. During the 20 days when the cheeses stand in a well-ventilated room, they become covered with mould. This is cleaned off and the cheeses removed to a cool, moist cellar to cure for another 15 days.

Tignard. A hard, blue veined cheese, which resembles Gex and Sassenage, made from ewe's or goat's milk in the Tigne Valley in Savoy.

INDIA

Dacca. Dacca is a small, medium-pressed cheese. Milk is clotted with rennet, the curd broken by hand and put into small wicker baskets and whey pressed out by weighted boards. After 10–14 days the cheeses are sufficiently dry and develop a thin coat of hardened cheese due to evaporation. They are smoked with wood or cow-dung, which has a sterilizing effect, and keep well for a month or two. Some people dislike the tarry flavour due to the smoking.

ITALY

Manteche. Manteche is flask-shaped and is a normal Provolone save that, sealed in the centre, is a small quantity of butter. The secret is jealously guarded of how the butter maintains its freshness for long periods and of how it resists melting during the working.

Pepato. This cheese is a spiced Pecorino made in Sicily. The curd is sometimes packed and cured in layers. Pepper is put between the layers or mixed with the curd in the vat.

NORWAY

Pultost. A soft fermented cheese made in all parts of Norway but particularly in the south-east. It is known by many different names, such as Knaost and Ramost, in different localities. Pultost is made from sour skimmed milk which is put in a kettle with 2 per cent of a lactic starter. The mixture of curd and whey is heated slowly and stirred continually until it reaches 130–140°F.

It is kept warm for several hours and stirred frequently to prevent the curd from matting. The whey is then drained and the curd broken up and salted. Sometimes caraway seeds are added. The curd is put in troughs and stirred occasionally. It can be eaten in a few days as a fresh cheese, but it may also be stored and ripened for later use.

PORTUGAL

Bola. A semi-hard cow's milk cheese of the Edam type and the most popular in Portugal.

SPAIN

Cebrero. Cheese named after Piedrafita del Cebrero. It looks like a short-stemmed wide-cap mushroom about 4 in. thick, from 14–16 in. diameter, varying in weight from 6–10 lb. The rind is pale yellow, the paste free from holes, of fine texture, softish, creamy, slightly sharp, with slight blue veining.

San Simon. Named after San Simon de la Cuesta in the province of Lugo where it is generally made. Shaped like a conical shell, the rind is very thin, shiny and dark yellow. Sizes vary from 2–10 lb. In flavor and consistency San Simon resembles Teta cheese.

Ulloa. Ulloa cheese comes from Galicia. Its paste is soft and reminds one of that of a ripe Camembert.

VENEZUELA

Cuajada. Cuajada (meaning "curdled") contains more cream than the similar Queso de Cincho and is generally wrapped in banana or maize leaves. Much eaten by country people.

Appendix II

ADDITIONAL CHEESE RECIPES

Evesham Flan

1¼ cups chopped asparagus
4 whole eggs and 4 yolks
⅓ pint milk
5 oz grated cheese
salt and pepper to taste

Line a flan ring with short paste and bake. Beat the eggs and yolks together. Add salt and pepper and pour in the milk. Put the cheese and asparagus in the flan shell, pour on the egg mixture and bake in a moderate oven (375°F., 190°C.).

Cheese Soufflé

3 tablespoons butter
4 tablespoons flour
¾ cup milk
salt and pepper
grated nutmeg
2 oz grated Gruyère or Parmesan
3 egg yolks
4 egg whites

Stir the milk into a white roux, composed of 3 tablespoons of butter and 4 tablespoons of flour. Season with salt, pepper and grated nutmeg; stir over a strong heat until boiling. Remove from the heat, add the cheese and the 3 egg yolks and, at the last moment and away from the fire, incorporate 4 egg whites stiffly beaten. Mix quickly, but do not beat. Fill a buttered soufflé dish with this mixture, filling only to within a finger's breadth from the top. Smooth over the surface of the soufflé, cook in a moderate oven for 20–25 minutes. Serve immediately. Season quite strongly to compensate for the weakening effect of adding egg whites.

Braised Endives with Cheese and Tarragon Sauce

This recipe goes very well as a hot accompaniment to any left-over cold meats, and is excellent with ham.

Belgian endives
1 oz butter
1 oz flour
1–1¼ cups cold milk
2 squares Demi Sel
tarragon
salt and pepper

Wash endives and remove any sad outside leaves; blanch for 2–3 minutes in boiling water, and then cook in a tin in the oven with a little stock until done (about 1 hour at medium heat—390°F., 200°C.).

Drain well, place in a warm dish and cover with the sauce made as follows. Melt 1 oz butter in a heavy saucepan, add 1 oz flour and cook gently until the roux is dry and crumbly but not brown. Add 1 cup of cold milk and leave on a very low flame, stirring occasionally with a wire whisk. You will finish up with a thickish Béchamel sauce. Add to this two squares of Demi Sel cheese and a few tarragon leaves and cook gently for 10 minutes. Adjust seasoning (plenty of salt and pepper) and, if too thick, add some of the drained liquor or some more milk to make a light creamy sauce.

Pimento Welsh Rarebit

Thick slice white bread
⅓ of an unripe Camembert
3 strips red pimento
3 strips green pimento
pepper
celery salt
butter
bacon fat or lard

Fry bread in bacon fat or lard until very crisp. Blend together in saucepan, over heat, the cheese, a knob of butter, pepper and celery salt. Spread mixture smoothly over the fried bread and put under a very hot broiler for 2 minutes. Remove, add pimentos in criss-cross fashion and return to broiler for another minute. Serve immediately.

Tartelettes Diane

    6 oz short pastry
    2 oz butter
    2 oz flour
    1¼ cups milk
    8 oz grated Cheddar cheese
    2 yolks of eggs
    mustard
    Worcestershire sauce
    chicken livers
    streaky bacon
    pickled walnuts

Line some deep tartlet molds with the short pastry and bake in a hot oven. Sauté the chicken livers and bacon in a little butter, cut into suitably sized pieces and place in bottom of the tartlets with a slice of pickled walnut. Make a sauce with the butter, flour and milk. Cook for 5 minutes and blend in the grated Cheddar cheese. Remove from fire and carefully add the yolks. Pour this mixture into the tartlets. Brown under broiler or in a hot oven. Serve very hot.

Hot Cheese and Tomato Quiche

for the pastry:
    ½ cup corn oil
    2 tablespoons iced water
    2 cups plain flour
    ½ level teaspoon salt

for the filling:
    12 spring onions, chopped
    ¾ lb tomatoes, skinned and sliced
    ½ tablespoon cornflour
    1 egg
    ⅓ pint milk
    ¼ pint light cream
    salt and pepper
    2 oz grated Cheddar cheese

Put the oil and iced water in a basin and blend well with a fork. Sift the flour and salt. Add gradually to the oil and water mixture to form a rollable dough. (Slightly more or less flour may be required). Roll out between two sheets of waxpaper. Line a 9 in. pie plate or flan ring, prick the bottom and sides of the shell with a fork and bake in a moderately hot oven (425°F., 220°C.) for 10 minutes.

Place the chopped spring onions in the pastry shell, saving a few for the garnish. Cover with slices of tomato, reserving some for the top of the quiche. Blend together the cornflour, beaten egg and milk. Stir in the cream, add salt and pepper and pour over the tomatoes and spring onions. Sprinkle with half the cheese. Bake for 45 minutes in a moderate oven (370°F., 190°C.). If the pastry becomes too brown, cover the edges with a little aluminum foil. Halfway through cooking, arrange the remaining sliced tomatoes on the top and sprinkle with the remaining cheese. Continue cooking. Garnish with chopped spring onions when cooked. Each quiche serves 8.

Baked Cheese Eggs

1 slice of Bel Paese cheese per person
butter
1 egg per person

Melt a little butter in the bottom of an individual ramequin dish. Put the slices of cheese in the dishes and break an egg into each. Put the dishes into one baking dish and cover. Bake in the oven until eggs are almost set.

Cheese Appetizer

$\frac{1}{2}$ lb cheese
1 oz butter
1 can tomato soup
2 eggs
crackers
1 saltspoon salt
$\frac{1}{2}$ saltspoon pepper

Cut the cheese into small pieces, then melt in a fireproof dish, add the butter, seasonings and tomato soup. When well mixed, add the eggs well beaten. Stir until it begins to thicken, and serve at once on buttered crackers.

Cheese Creams

    2 heaped tablespoons grated cheese
    1 cup half-set aspic jelly
    1 cup whipping cream
    1 tablespoon chopped parsley
    salt
    pepper
    red pepper

Beat the cream until stiff and stir in the cheese; add the aspic jelly and the seasonings. Divide into china ramequins; when set, sprinkle with a little chopped parsley. Serve very cold.

Cheese Croustades

    bread
    breadcrumbs (about 1 oz)
    2 oz grated cheese
    1 tablespoon milk
    1 tablespoon melted butter
    1 egg yolk
    salt
    pepper and cayenne

Cut the bread into pieces about 2 in. by $\frac{1}{2}$ in. and hollow out the middle. Mix together cheese, breadcrumbs, milk, melted butter, egg yolk, salt, pepper and cayenne. Fry the croustades in fat or oil until golden, pile the cheese mixture in until you have a cone, put in the oven to brown and serve hot.

Cheese Feathers

    $\frac{1}{2}$ cup cold water
    1 tablespoon butter
    $\frac{1}{4}$ cup flour
    $1\frac{1}{2}$ oz grated cheese
    1 whole egg and half a yolk
    pepper

Boil the water and butter together, add flour, stirring all the time, remove from fire and add egg and cheese. Drop with a teaspoon, one by one, into boiling fat till pale brown. Serve with grated cheese.

(Oriana Haynes, *Cooking and Curing*).

Cheese Puffs

2 tablespoons butter
4 tablespoons flour
4 tablespoons grated cheese
2 eggs
1 cupful water
½ teaspoon salt
pinch of pepper

Wet the flour in a little of the water until it forms a smooth paste, and add the cheese, salt and pepper. Place the rest of the water and the butter in a saucepan and when boiling, add the flour mixture. Cook 3 minutes, stirring all the time; remove the mixture from the fire and set aside to cool. When cold, add the eggs unbeaten, one at a time, and beat the batter at least 10 minutes. Butter a baking tin lightly, and drop the mixture into it, using a heaping teaspoon for each puff, and leaving considerable space between them, as they increase threefold in size. Bake 20 minutes, and serve hot. Sometimes a plain cream sauce or a brown sauce is served with these puffs.

(*Happy Kitchens Magazine*, 1885).

Crab and Cheese Toasts

1 can crabmeat
grated cheese
lemon juice
tarragon vinegar
breadcrumbs
mustard
butter
cayenne pepper
salt and pepper
buttered toast

Make the crab into a pulp. Add a small piece of butter, salt, pepper, mustard, cayenne and a squeeze of lemon. Wet down with a little tarragon vinegar and add breadcrumbs if too wet. Spread mixture on toast. Sprinkle with lots of grated cheese, add a bit of butter on top, and bake in a very hot oven for a few minutes. Serve very quickly. When using very fresh crab, pound the coral with the meat.

Pruneaux Farcis au Fromage

stewed prunes
grated Cheddar or Gruyère cheese
mayonnaise
lettuce

Choose good prunes, stew them until tender (but not broken), drain them and let them cool. Then remove the stones carefully without breaking the prunes in pieces. Moisten grated cheese with thick mayonnaise. Season the mixture well and put a little into each prune, giving each its original form. Serve them on small leaves of round lettuce, pouring over a little more mayonnaise if desired. Sprinkle with finely-chopped parsley.

(James Tait, *You and Your Kitchen*, 1903).

Cheese Roulettes

4 oz St. Ivel cheese
3 oz white breadcrumbs
2 egg yolks
seasoning
fat for frying

Mix the cheese and breadcrumbs (fine and soft) to a smooth paste, until the mixture is heated; spread on a buttered plate. When cool, make into roulettes; dip each in beaten egg yolks, or thin frying batter. Fry in hot fat to a delicate brown. Drain, dish and garnish with fried parsley.

(*Happy Kitchens Magazine*, 1885).

Semolina Cheese

pepper to taste
1½ cups scalded milk
2 cups grated Cheddar cheese
1 teaspoon grated Parmesan cheese
4 tablespoons of semolina

Boil the milk, and when boiling add semolina. Stir till smooth and thick, add cheese and pepper and cook slowly for 5 minutes. Turn into dish or individual ramequins. Sprinkle a little cheese on the top and dot with butter. Brown under broiler.

(I never tire of this. T.A.L.).

Ramequins Soufflé

1 oz butter
1 tablespoon flour
1¼ cups milk
½ lb grated Parmesan cheese
8 egg yolks
8 egg whites
salt and pepper
little powdered sugar
¼ pint cream

Melt the butter; mix in the flour and a little salt; stir for a few minutes over the fire. Have ready boiled 1¼ cups milk and ¼ pint cream. Pour this on the butter and flour by degrees, and work it perfectly smooth. Take the pan off the fire and add grated Parmesan cheese, a little pepper, a very little powdered sugar, the yolks of 8 eggs and the whites of 2 well beaten. When well mixed, add the other 6 whites, beaten to a froth. It should then be about the consistency of cream. Fill individual buttered ramequins not quite to the top, and bake in a slow oven for 18 minutes. (*Happy Kitchens Magazine,* 1885).

Soupe à l'Oignon Gratinée (France)

3 or 4 large onions
1 tablespoon butter
1 tablespoon flour
salt and pepper
5 cups meat stock
French bread
grated cheese

Peel the onions and slice them thinly. Warm the butter in a heavy saucepan, and cook the onions gently until they are translucent and golden brown. Stir in the flour, season with salt and pepper, and add the stock. Bring to the boil and simmer for 20 minutes. Slice the bread thinly and dry it in the oven. Have ready and warm an individual bowl for each guest, add a slice or two of the bread to each, pour the soup over the bread, sprinkle a generous layer of grated cheese on top of the bread and brown under a very hot broiler before serving immediately.

Zuppa Pavese (Italy)

4 eggs
5 cups chicken, meat or vegetable consommé
French bread
butter
grated cheese

Heat the consommé. Fry the slices of bread in butter; allow two or three slices of bread to each bowl of soup. Poach the eggs in the consommé, drain them and slip them into the heated bowls. Pour the consommé over the eggs. Sprinkle a little grated cheese over each slice of bread and arrange round the egg. Serve more cheese separately.

Edam and Bacon Sandwich

bread
unsalted butter
bacon
tomatoes
Edam cheese
salt
paprika

Cut bread into slices 1 in. thick, toast lightly, brush with butter. On each slice lay a strip of broiled bacon. Place a slice of tomato on the bacon, sprinkle generously with grated Edam, season with salt and paprika. Put in the oven until the Edam has melted. Ham may be used in place of bacon.

Cheese and Breadcrumbs

1 cup grated cheese
1 cup milk
1 cup breadcrumbs
1 heaping teaspoon butter
3 eggs
salt and red pepper

Scald the milk and butter; remove from the stove and add the cheese, breadcrumbs and seasonings. Beat up the eggs and add them lightly. Pour into a buttered fireproof dish and bake for 20 minutes. Serve at once.

Cheese and Olive Tart à la Layton

shortcrust pastry
thin slices of Gruyère
pitted olives
4 egg yolks
milk
grated cheese
butter

Line a baking pan with pastry. Smear with dabs of butter and arrange slices of Gruyère and olives. Cover with custard made from the egg yolks mixed with a little milk. Put some more butter on top and sprinkle with grated cheese. Bake in a quick oven.

Cheese Pudding

1¼ cups milk
3 oz grated cheese
3 oz breadcrumbs
2 eggs, separated
pepper and salt

Boil the milk, and add to it the grated cheese. When all is dissolved pour over the breadcrumbs. Stir all together nicely, pour into a basin, and when cooled a little, add the yolks of eggs and seasoning. Whip the whites of eggs till very stiff, stir them lightly into the mixture, pour all into a greased pie dish, and bake for 20 minutes in a good steady oven. Serve immediately.
(*Happy Kitchens Magazine*, 1885).

Mushrooms and Cheese on Toast

olive oil or butter
1½ lb mushrooms
tomato paste
3 tablespoons grated cheese
salt and pepper

Peel mushrooms and slice thinly. Fry slowly in oil or butter for about 15 minutes with salt and pepper. Then add 1 tablespoon tomato paste which has been dissolved in 2 tablespoons of stock or boiling water. Cook slowly for 5 minutes. Add grated cheese and continue to cook slowly for 10 minutes. Serve on toast.

Cheese Baba

2 oz butter
2 tablespoons flour
$\frac{1}{2}$ cup of milk
2 tablespoons cream
4 eggs, separated
4 tablespoons grated cheese
salt

Make a sauce with the butter, flour, milk and cream. Cook for a few minutes and then remove from heat and add egg yolks, grated cheese and a pinch of salt. Fold in the beaten egg whites and turn out onto a fireproof dish. Steam for about 1 hour and turn out on-to ovenproof dish. Sprinkle with grated cheese and put in the oven for about 20 minutes to brown top.

Cheese Pudding (Devonshire)

slices of thin bread and butter
4 oz grated cheese
2 eggs
$2\frac{1}{2}$ cups milk
seasoning

Grease a $1\frac{1}{2}$ pint ovenproof dish. Cover the bottom with slices of bread and butter—buttered side up. Sprinkle over them a layer of grated cheese. Repeat the layers until the dish is full. Reserve a little cheese for sprinkling over top. Break the eggs into a basin, add salt and pepper, beat well and mix with the milk. Pour this custard over the bread, and let it stand for at least 30 minutes. Bake in a moderate oven for 30–40 minutes, allowing the top to become brown and crisp. Serve very hot.

Cheese Omelette

5 eggs
2 oz grated Parmesan cheese
1 oz Gruyère cheese
pinch of salt
2 pinches pepper

Prepare the eggs as for a plain omelette. Mix with them 2 oz of finely grated Parmesan cheese, a small pinch of salt, and two pinches of pepper. Fry the omelette in the usual way, and before folding it over strew the finely-minced Gruyère cheese upon it. Fold, and serve immediately. Time, 4 or 5 minutes to fry. Sufficient for 3 persons.

(*Shilling Cookery*, Grant Richards Publishers, 1904).

Macaroni, Eggs and Cheese

    4 hard boiled eggs (chopped)
    1 cup cooked elbow macaroni
    ¾ cup grated cheese
    2½ cups white sauce
    onion juice
    salt and paprika
    breadcrumbs

Mix all the ingredients together lightly and then put into a greased bowl or fireproof dish. Cover the top with buttered crumbs and bake in a moderate oven until brown.

Camembert Savoury

    1 medium ripe Camembert
    1¼ cups Bechamel or white sauce
    1 egg yolk
    2 tablespoons flour
    1 egg
    1 tablespoon milk
    1 teaspoon olive oil
    ½ cup white breadcrumbs
    enough fat for deep frying
    2 oz Parmesan cheese (finely grated)
    salt, pepper and a dash of Tobasco sauce

Remove rind from cheese and put through mouli or fine sieve. Make white sauce, season and cool. Blend in Camembert, egg yolk and tobasco until smooth. Shape into little balls about the size of a small plum on a floured board. Beat egg with milk and oil. Dip cheese balls into this mixture, roll in breadcrumbs and fry in deep fat until golden brown. Dust with Parmesan cheese and serve hot.

Cheese Toasts with Chicken Liver

3 chicken livers
1 anchovy fillet
stock
grated cheese
breadcrumbs
salt and paprika
butter

Fry livers in a little butter with salt and paprika. Chop up and mix with anchovy in oil. Put a tablespoon of stock in a saucepan and cook liver mixture until it becomes like a spread. Spread mixture on to pieces of buttered toast and top with grated cheese mixed with breadcrumbs. Top with butter and place in oven to brown.

Croûtes à la St. Ivel

St. Ivel cheese
2 tablespoons cream
1 teaspoon grated horseradish
seasonings
stale loaf of bread

Mix half a St. Ivel cheese with the cream and horseradish, season with a pinch of paprika and a few drops of tarragon vinegar. Cut some thin slices from a stale loaf of bread, stamp a sufficient number of rounds, $1\frac{1}{2}$-in. diameter, fry in butter and drain. Spread them rather thickly, on one side only, with the above cheese mixture. Place them on a baking sheet in a hot oven for about 5 minutes. Dish. Garnish with sprigs of parsley and lemon slices. Serve hot.
(*Geraldine's Home Cookery*, 1906).

Way Down South Rarebit

2 eggs (lightly beaten)
3 cups cooked tomatoes
$1\frac{1}{2}$ tablepoons sugar
4 cups grated cheese
$1\frac{1}{2}$ tablespoons butter
1 shredded onion

big pinch salt
good shake pepper

Get a good thick frying pan and fry the onion in the butter. Add the tomatoes and the sugar. Never let this mixture boil, and gradually add the cheese, stirring so that it melts. Add the seasonings and remove mixture from heat. Stir in the eggs and serve piping hot on fried bread.

Punjab Curry Rarebit

    1 tablespoon mango chutney
    3 cups grated Leicester cheese
    ½ teaspoon curry powder
    1 tablespoon cornflour
    2 cups milk
    2 finely shredded onions
    1 tablespoon tomato purée

Melt the cornflour in the milk until it is well cooked and begins to thicken. When it does, pour in the cheese, curry powder, mango chutney and onions. Stir well with a wooden spoon until a first-rate blending has taken place. Then stir in the tomato purée. Stir again rather more vigorously this time and serve on thick hot buttered toast.

Käseschnitte (Austrian Cheese Slices)

    1 tablespoon butter
    1 tablespoon flour
    4 tablespoons milk
    1 egg
    salt and pepper
    2 tablespoons Parmesan or Cheddar cheese
    2 tablespoons Dutch cheese
    rolls.

Warm the butter and stir in the flour to make a soft roux. Cook gently, but do not brown. Add the milk, previously warmed, and season. Take the pan away from the heat and stir in the cheese and egg. Cut the rolls into thin slices, and spread with the cheese mixture. Sprinkle more grated cheese on top. Brown in a very hot oven and serve with clear soups.

Dervishes Delight

3 ozs red Algerian wine
1 cup mulligatawny soup
1 tablespoon flour
½ teaspoon salt
2 eggs (beaten)
1 small shredded onion
¼ teaspoon dry mustard
2 tablespoons butter
3 cups grated Cheddar cheese

Put the butter in a frying pan and cook the onion until it begins to
turn, then put in the flour, the wine, the soup and the mustard.
Next stir in the cheese and cook again. Finally add the eggs and
continue stirring until the mixture gets lovely and unctuous.
Serve on soft buttered toast.

Tomato and Cheese Savoury

½ lb tomatoes
1 onion
1 oz butter
½ oz grated Parmesan cheese
2 eggs
rounds of toast
pepper and salt

First slice the tomatoes and onion thinly and fry gently in the
butter until cooked. Then add the Parmesan and seasonings of
pepper and salt. Beat 2 eggs thoroughly, pour into the tomato,
etc., and stir gently till all is quite the consistency of a smooth
paste. Pile on hot buttered toast, and serve very hot.
(*Isobel's Home Cookery*, 1903–5).

Cheese Straws

1½ cups flour
approximately ½ cup butter
5 oz grated Parmesan and fresh Cheddar cheese
salt
pepper
cayenne pepper
egg yolk

Sift the flour, add seasoning. Rub in the butter with quick, cool hands, and add the grated cheese, and enough egg yolk to make a stiff paste. Flour the board well and roll out to about a quarter of an inch thick. The finished pastry will be very breakable and fragile so do not make the straws too thin. Cut into straws, and if liked some rings as well. Bake in a moderate oven (320°F., 160–170°C.). As a savoury, slip straws through the rings and serve very hot with plenty of English mustard. Or leave to cool and serve with drinks before dinner.

Macaroni with Cheese

$\frac{1}{4}$ lb macaroni
$\frac{1}{4}$ lb grated cheese
1 tablespoon butter
1 tablespoon flour
$1\frac{1}{4}$ cups milk
seasonings

Boil the macaroni in salted water for about 20 minutes, or until tender enough to cut with a fork. Drain. Melt butter in a saucepan, stir in the flour, then add milk and stir till well boiled. Remove from heat and stir in half the grated cheese and the macaroni; season with pepper, cayenne pepper, salt and a little mustard if liked. Turn all out on to a buttered dish, sprinkle the remainder of the cheese on top and bake in a quick oven until nicely brown.
(*Happy Kitchens Magazine*, 1885).

Cheese Bars

flaky pastry
5 oz grated cheese
1 tomato
1 egg
cayenne or mustard to season

Line a flat tin with flaky pastry. Mix all the other ingredients together (leaving a little white of egg), spread the mixture on the pastry. Brush over with the white of egg and cook for about 20 minutes in a fairly hot oven. Cut into finger lengths and serve hot.
(*Cornish Fare*)

INDEX OF CHEESES

A CATALOGUE OF SELECTED DOVER BOOKS
IN ALL FIELDS OF INTEREST

A CATALOGUE OF SELECTED DOVER BOOKS
IN ALL FIELDS OF INTEREST

AMERICA'S OLD MASTERS, James T. Flexner. Four men emerged unexpectedly from provincial 18th century America to leadership in European art: Benjamin West, J. S. Copley, C. R. Peale, Gilbert Stuart. Brilliant coverage of lives and contributions. Revised, 1967 edition. 69 plates. 365pp. of text.
21806-6 Paperbound $3.00

FIRST FLOWERS OF OUR WILDERNESS: AMERICAN PAINTING, THE COLONIAL PERIOD, James T. Flexner. Painters, and regional painting traditions from earliest Colonial times up to the emergence of Copley, West and Peale Sr., Foster, Gustavus Hesselius, Feke, John Smibert and many anonymous painters in the primitive manner. Engaging presentation, with 162 illustrations. xxii + 368pp.
22180-6 Paperbound $3.50

THE LIGHT OF DISTANT SKIES: AMERICAN PAINTING, 1760-1835, James T. Flexner. The great generation of early American painters goes to Europe to learn and to teach: West, Copley, Gilbert Stuart and others. Allston, Trumbull, Morse; also contemporary American painters—primitives, derivatives, academics—who remained in America. 102 illustrations. xiii + 306pp. 22179-2 Paperbound $3.50

A HISTORY OF THE RISE AND PROGRESS OF THE ARTS OF DESIGN IN THE UNITED STATES, William Dunlap. Much the richest mine of information on early American painters, sculptors, architects, engravers, miniaturists, etc. The only source of information for scores of artists, the major primary source for many others. Unabridged reprint of rare original 1834 edition, with new introduction by James T. Flexner, and 394 new illustrations. Edited by Rita Weiss. 6⅝ x 9⅝.
21695-0, 21696-9, 21697-7 Three volumes, Paperbound $13.50

EPOCHS OF CHINESE AND JAPANESE ART, Ernest F. Fenollosa. From primitive Chinese art to the 20th century, thorough history, explanation of every important art period and form, including Japanese woodcuts; main stress on China and Japan, but Tibet, Korea also included. Still unexcelled for its detailed, rich coverage of cultural background, aesthetic elements, diffusion studies, particularly of the historical period. 2nd, 1913 edition. 242 illustrations. lii + 439pp. of text.
20364-6, 20365-4 Two volumes, Paperbound $6.00

THE GENTLE ART OF MAKING ENEMIES, James A. M. Whistler. Greatest wit of his day deflates Oscar Wilde, Ruskin, Swinburne; strikes back at inane critics, exhibitions, art journalism; aesthetics of impressionist revolution in most striking form. Highly readable classic by great painter. Reproduction of edition designed by Whistler. Introduction by Alfred Werner. xxxvi + 334pp.
21875-9 Paperbound $2.50

VISUAL ILLUSIONS: THEIR CAUSES, CHARACTERISTICS, AND APPLICATIONS, Matthew Luckiesh. Thorough description and discussion of optical illusion, geometric and perspective, particularly; size and shape distortions, illusions of color, of motion; natural illusions; use of illusion in art and magic, industry, etc. Most useful today with op art, also for classical art. Scores of effects illustrated. Introduction by William H. Ittleson. 100 illustrations. xxi + 252pp.

21530-X Paperbound $2.00

A HANDBOOK OF ANATOMY FOR ART STUDENTS, Arthur Thomson. Thorough, virtually exhaustive coverage of skeletal structure, musculature, etc. Full text, supplemented by anatomical diagrams and drawings and by photographs of undraped figures. Unique in its comparison of male and female forms, pointing out differences of contour, texture, form. 211 figures, 40 drawings, 86 photographs. xx + 459pp. 5⅜ x 8⅜.

21163-0 Paperbound $3.50

150 MASTERPIECES OF DRAWING, Selected by Anthony Toney. Full page reproductions of drawings from the early 16th to the end of the 18th century, all beautifully reproduced: Rembrandt, Michelangelo, Dürer, Fragonard, Urs, Graf, Wouwerman, many others. First-rate browsing book, model book for artists. xviii + 150pp. 8⅜ x 11¼.

21032-4 Paperbound $2.50

THE LATER WORK OF AUBREY BEARDSLEY, Aubrey Beardsley. Exotic, erotic, ironic masterpieces in full maturity: Comedy Ballet, Venus and Tannhauser, Pierrot, Lysistrata, Rape of the Lock, Savoy material, Ali Baba, Volpone, etc. This material revolutionized the art world, and is still powerful, fresh, brilliant. With *The Early Work,* all Beardsley's finest work. 174 plates, 2 in color. xiv + 176pp. 8⅛ x 11.

21817-1 Paperbound $3.00

DRAWINGS OF REMBRANDT, Rembrandt van Rijn. Complete reproduction of fabulously rare edition by Lippmann and Hofstede de Groot, completely reedited, updated, improved by Prof. Seymour Slive, Fogg Museum. Portraits, Biblical sketches, landscapes, Oriental types, nudes, episodes from classical mythology—All Rembrandt's fertile genius. Also selection of drawings by his pupils and followers. "Stunning volumes," *Saturday Review.* 550 illustrations. lxxviii + 552pp. 9⅛ x 12¼.

21485-0, 21486-9 Two volumes, Paperbound $10.00

THE DISASTERS OF WAR, Francisco Goya. One of the masterpieces of Western civilization—83 etchings that record Goya's shattering, bitter reaction to the Napoleonic war that swept through Spain after the insurrection of 1808 and to war in general. Reprint of the first edition, with three additional plates from Boston's Museum of Fine Arts. All plates facsimile size. Introduction by Philip Hofer, Fogg Museum. v + 97pp. 9⅜ x 8¼.

21872-4 Paperbound $2.00

GRAPHIC WORKS OF ODILON REDON. Largest collection of Redon's graphic works ever assembled: 172 lithographs, 28 etchings and engravings, 9 drawings. These include some of his most famous works. All the plates from *Odilon Redon: oeuvre graphique complet,* plus additional plates. New introduction and caption translations by Alfred Werner. 209 illustrations. xxvii + 209pp. 9⅛ x 12¼.

21966-8 Paperbound $4.00

DESIGN BY ACCIDENT; A BOOK OF "ACCIDENTAL EFFECTS" FOR ARTISTS AND DESIGNERS, James F. O'Brien. Create your own unique, striking, imaginative effects by "controlled accident" interaction of materials: paints and lacquers, oil and water based paints, splatter, crackling materials, shatter, similar items. Everything you do will be different; first book on this limitless art, so useful to both fine artist and commercial artist. Full instructions. 192 plates showing "accidents," 8 in color. viii + 215pp. 8⅜ x 11¼. 21942-9 Paperbound $3.50

THE BOOK OF SIGNS, Rudolf Koch. Famed German type designer draws 493 beautiful symbols: religious, mystical, alchemical, imperial, property marks, runes, etc. Remarkable fusion of traditional and modern. Good for suggestions of timelessness, smartness, modernity. Text. vi + 104pp. 6⅛ x 9¼. 20162-7 Paperbound $1.25

HISTORY OF INDIAN AND INDONESIAN ART, Ananda K. Coomaraswamy. An unabridged republication of one of the finest books by a great scholar in Eastern art. Rich in descriptive material, history, social backgrounds; Sunga reliefs, Rajput paintings, Gupta temples, Burmese frescoes, textiles, jewelry, sculpture, etc. 400 photos. viii + 423pp. 6⅜ x 9¾. 21436-2 Paperbound $5.00

PRIMITIVE ART, Franz Boas. America's foremost anthropologist surveys textiles, ceramics, woodcarving, basketry, metalwork, etc.; patterns, technology, creation of symbols, style origins. All areas of world, but very full on Northwest Coast Indians. More than 350 illustrations of baskets, boxes, totem poles, weapons, etc. 378 pp. 20025-6 Paperbound $3.00

THE GENTLEMAN AND CABINET MAKER'S DIRECTOR, Thomas Chippendale. Full reprint (third edition, 1762) of most influential furniture book of all time, by master cabinetmaker. 200 plates, illustrating chairs, sofas, mirrors, tables, cabinets, plus 24 photographs of surviving pieces. Biographical introduction by N. Bienenstock. vi + 249pp. 9⅞ x 12¾. 21601-2 Paperbound $4.00

AMERICAN ANTIQUE FURNITURE, Edgar G. Miller, Jr. The basic coverage of all American furniture before 1840. Individual chapters cover type of furniture— clocks, tables, sideboards, etc.—chronologically, with inexhaustible wealth of data. More than 2100 photographs, all identified, commented on. Essential to all early American collectors. Introduction by H. E. Keyes. vi + 1106pp. 7⅞ x 10¾. 21599-7, 21600-4 Two volumes, Paperbound $11.00

PENNSYLVANIA DUTCH AMERICAN FOLK ART, Henry J. Kauffman. 279 photos, 28 drawings of tulipware, Fraktur script, painted tinware, toys, flowered furniture, quilts, samplers, hex signs, house interiors, etc. Full descriptive text. Excellent for tourist, rewarding for designer, collector. Map. 146pp. 7⅞ x 10¾. 21205-X Paperbound $2.50

EARLY NEW ENGLAND GRAVESTONE RUBBINGS, Edmund V. Gillon, Jr. 43 photographs, 226 carefully reproduced rubbings show heavily symbolic, sometimes macabre early gravestones, up to early 19th century. Remarkable early American primitive art, occasionally strikingly beautiful; always powerful. Text. xxvi + 207pp. 8⅜ x 11¼. 21380-3 Paperbound $3.50

ALPHABETS AND ORNAMENTS, Ernst Lehner. Well-known pictorial source for decorative alphabets, script examples, cartouches, frames, decorative title pages, calligraphic initials, borders, similar material. 14th to 19th century, mostly European. Useful in almost any graphic arts designing, varied styles. 750 illustrations. 256pp. 7 x 10. 21905-4 Paperbound $4.00

PAINTING: A CREATIVE APPROACH, Norman Colquhoun. For the beginner simple guide provides an instructive approach to painting: major stumbling blocks for beginner; overcoming them, technical points; paints and pigments; oil painting; watercolor and other media and color. New section on "plastic" paints. Glossary. Formerly *Paint Your Own Pictures*. 221pp. 22000-1 Paperbound $1.75

THE ENJOYMENT AND USE OF COLOR, Walter Sargent. Explanation of the relations between colors themselves and between colors in nature and art, including hundreds of little-known facts about color values, intensities, effects of high and low illumination, complementary colors. Many practical hints for painters, references to great masters. 7 color plates, 29 illustrations. x + 274pp.
20944-X Paperbound $2.75

THE NOTEBOOKS OF LEONARDO DA VINCI, compiled and edited by Jean Paul Richter. 1566 extracts from original manuscripts reveal the full range of Leonardo's versatile genius: all his writings on painting, sculpture, architecture, anatomy, astronomy, geography, topography, physiology, mining, music, etc., in both Italian and English, with 186 plates of manuscript pages and more than 500 additional drawings. Includes studies for the Last Supper, the lost Sforza monument, and other works. Total of xlvii + 866pp. 7⅞ x 10¾.
22572-0, 22573-9 Two volumes, Paperbound $10.00

MONTGOMERY WARD CATALOGUE OF 1895. Tea gowns, yards of flannel and pillow-case lace, stereoscopes, books of gospel hymns, the New Improved Singer Sewing Machine, side saddles, milk skimmers, straight-edged razors, high-button shoes, spittoons, and on and on . . . listing some 25,000 items, practically all illustrated. Essential to the shoppers of the 1890's, it is our truest record of the spirit of the period. Unaltered reprint of Issue No. 57, Spring and Summer 1895. Introduction by Boris Emmet. Innumerable illustrations. xiii + 624pp. 8½ x 11⅝.
22377-9 Paperbound $6.95

THE CRYSTAL PALACE EXHIBITION ILLUSTRATED CATALOGUE (LONDON, 1851). One of the wonders of the modern world—the Crystal Palace Exhibition in which all the nations of the civilized world exhibited their achievements in the arts and sciences—presented in an equally important illustrated catalogue. More than 1700 items pictured with accompanying text—ceramics, textiles, cast-iron work, carpets, pianos, sleds, razors, wall-papers, billiard tables, beehives, silverware and hundreds of other artifacts—represent the focal point of Victorian culture in the Western World. Probably the largest collection of Victorian decorative art ever assembled—indispensable for antiquarians and designers. Unabridged republication of the Art-Journal Catalogue of the Great Exhibition of 1851, with all terminal essays. New introduction by John Gloag, F.S.A. xxxiv + 426pp. 9 x 12.
22503-8 Paperbound $4.50

A History of Costume, Carl Köhler. Definitive history, based on surviving pieces of clothing primarily, and paintings, statues, etc. secondarily. Highly readable text, supplemented by 594 illustrations of costumes of the ancient Mediterranean peoples, Greece and Rome, the Teutonic prehistoric period; costumes of the Middle Ages, Renaissance, Baroque, 18th and 19th centuries. Clear, measured patterns are provided for many clothing articles. Approach is practical throughout. Enlarged by Emma von Sichart. 464pp.   21030-8 Paperbound $3.50

Oriental Rugs, Antique and Modern, Walter A. Hawley. A complete and authoritative treatise on the Oriental rug—where they are made, by whom and how, designs and symbols, characteristics in detail of the six major groups, how to distinguish them and how to buy them. Detailed technical data is provided on periods, weaves, warps, wefts, textures, sides, ends and knots, although no technical background is required for an understanding. 11 color plates, 80 halftones, 4 maps. vi + 320pp. 6⅛ x 9⅛.   22366-3 Paperbound $5.00

Ten Books on Architecture, Vitruvius. By any standards the most important book on architecture ever written. Early Roman discussion of aesthetics of building, construction methods, orders, sites, and every other aspect of architecture has inspired, instructed architecture for about 2,000 years. Stands behind Palladio, Michelangelo, Bramante, Wren, countless others. Definitive Morris H. Morgan translation. 68 illustrations. xii + 331pp.   20645-9 Paperbound $3.00

The Four Books of Architecture, Andrea Palladio. Translated into every major Western European language in the two centuries following its publication in 1570, this has been one of the most influential books in the history of architecture. Complete reprint of the 1738 Isaac Ware edition. New introduction by Adolf Placzek, Columbia Univ. 216 plates. xxii + 110pp. of text. 9½ x 12¾.
                           21308-0 Clothbound $10.00

Sticks and Stones: A Study of American Architecture and Civilization, Lewis Mumford.One of the great classics of American cultural history. American architecture from the medieval-inspired earliest forms to the early 20th century; evolution of structure and style, and reciprocal influences on environment. 21 photographic illustrations. 238pp.   20202-X Paperbound $2.00

The American Builder's Companion, Asher Benjamin. The most widely used early 19th century architectural style and source book, for colonial up into Greek Revival periods. Extensive development of geometry of carpentering, construction of sashes, frames, doors, stairs; plans and elevations of domestic and other buildings. Hundreds of thousands of houses were built according to this book, now invaluable to historians, architects, restorers, etc. 1827 edition. 59 plates. 114pp. 7⅞ x 10¾.
                           22236-5 Paperbound $3.50

Dutch Houses in the Hudson Valley Before 1776, Helen Wilkinson Reynolds. The standard survey of the Dutch colonial house and outbuildings, with constructional features, decoration, and local history associated with individual homesteads. Introduction by Franklin D. Roosevelt. Map. 150 illustrations. 469pp. 6⅝ x 9¼.   21469-9 Paperbound $4.00

THE ARCHITECTURE OF COUNTRY HOUSES, Andrew J. Downing. Together with Vaux's *Villas and Cottages* this is the basic book for Hudson River Gothic architecture of the middle Victorian period. Full, sound discussions of general aspects of housing, architecture, style, decoration, furnishing, together with scores of detailed house plans, illustrations of specific buildings, accompanied by full text. Perhaps the most influential single American architectural book. 1850 edition. Introduction by J. Stewart Johnson. 321 figures, 34 architectural designs. xvi + 560pp.
22003-6 Paperbound $4.00

LOST EXAMPLES OF COLONIAL ARCHITECTURE, John Mead Howells. Full-page photographs of buildings that have disappeared or been so altered as to be denatured, including many designed by major early American architects. 245 plates. xvii + 248pp. 7⅞ x 10¾. 21143-6 Paperbound $3.50

DOMESTIC ARCHITECTURE OF THE AMERICAN COLONIES AND OF THE EARLY REPUBLIC, Fiske Kimball. Foremost architect and restorer of Williamsburg and Monticello covers nearly 200 homes between 1620-1825. Architectural details, construction, style features, special fixtures, floor plans, etc. Generally considered finest work in its area. 219 illustrations of houses, doorways, windows, capital mantels. xx + 314pp. 7⅞ x 10¾. 21743-4 Paperbound $4.00

EARLY AMERICAN ROOMS: 1650-1858, edited by Russell Hawes Kettell. Tour of 12 rooms, each representative of a different era in American history and each furnished, decorated, designed and occupied in the style of the era. 72 plans and elevations, 8-page color section, etc., show fabrics, wall papers, arrangements, etc. Full descriptive text. xvii + 200pp. of text. 8⅜ x 11¼.
21633-0 Paperbound $5.00

THE FITZWILLIAM VIRGINAL BOOK, edited by J. Fuller Maitland and W. B. Squire. Full modern printing of famous early 17th-century ms. volume of 300 works by Morley, Byrd, Bull, Gibbons, etc. For piano or other modern keyboard instrument; easy to read format. xxxvi + 938pp. 8⅜ x 11.
21068-5, 21069-3 Two volumes, Paperbound $10.00

KEYBOARD MUSIC, Johann Sebastian Bach. Bach Gesellschaft edition. A rich selection of Bach's masterpieces for the harpsichord: the six English Suites, six French Suites, the six Partitas (Clavierübung part I), the Goldberg Variations (Clavierübung part IV), the fifteen Two-Part Inventions and the fifteen Three-Part Sinfonias. Clearly reproduced on large sheets with ample margins; eminently playable. vi + 312pp. 8⅛ x 11. 22360-4 Paperbound $5.00

THE MUSIC OF BACH: AN INTRODUCTION, Charles Sanford Terry. A fine, nontechnical introduction to Bach's music, both instrumental and vocal. Covers organ music, chamber music, passion music, other types. Analyzes themes, developments, innovations. x + 114pp. 21075-8 Paperbound $1.25

BEETHOVEN AND HIS NINE SYMPHONIES, Sir George Grove. Noted British musicologist provides best history, analysis, commentary on symphonies. Very thorough, rigorously accurate; necessary to both advanced student and amateur music lover. 436 musical passages. vii + 407 pp. 20334-4 Paperbound $2.75

JOHANN SEBASTIAN BACH, Philipp Spitta. One of the great classics of musicology, this definitive analysis of Bach's music (and life) has never been surpassed. Lucid, nontechnical analyses of hundreds of pieces (30 pages devoted to St. Matthew Passion, 26 to B Minor Mass). Also includes major analysis of 18th-century music. 450 musical examples. 40-page musical supplement. Total of xx + 1799pp.

(EUK) 22278-0, 22279-9 Two volumes, Clothbound $17.50

MOZART AND HIS PIANO CONCERTOS, Cuthbert Girdlestone. The only full-length study of an important area of Mozart's creativity. Provides detailed analyses of all 23 concertos, traces inspirational sources. 417 musical examples. Second edition. 509pp. 21271-8 Paperbound $3.50

THE PERFECT WAGNERITE: A COMMENTARY ON THE NIBLUNG'S RING, George Bernard Shaw. Brilliant and still relevant criticism in remarkable essays on Wagner's Ring cycle, Shaw's ideas on political and social ideology behind the plots, role of Leitmotifs, vocal requisites, etc. Prefaces. xxi + 136pp.

(USO) 21707-8 Paperbound $1.50

DON GIOVANNI, W. A. Mozart. Complete libretto, modern English translation; biographies of composer and librettist; accounts of early performances and critical reaction. Lavishly illustrated. All the material you need to understand and appreciate this great work. Dover Opera Guide and Libretto Series; translated and introduced by Ellen Bleiler. 92 illustrations. 209pp.

21134-7 Paperbound $2.00

HIGH FIDELITY SYSTEMS: A LAYMAN'S GUIDE, Roy F. Allison. All the basic information you need for setting up your own audio system: high fidelity and stereo record players, tape records, F.M. Connections, adjusting tone arm, cartridge, checking needle alignment, positioning speakers, phasing speakers, adjusting hums, trouble-shooting, maintenance, and similar topics. Enlarged 1965 edition. More than 50 charts, diagrams, photos. iv + 91pp. 21514-8 Paperbound $1.25

REPRODUCTION OF SOUND, Edgar Villchur. Thorough coverage for laymen of high fidelity systems, reproducing systems in general, needles, amplifiers, preamps, loudspeakers, feedback, explaining physical background. "A rare talent for making technicalities vividly comprehensible," R. Darrell, *High Fidelity.* 69 figures. iv + 92pp. 21515-6 Paperbound $1.25

HEAR ME TALKIN' TO YA: THE STORY OF JAZZ AS TOLD BY THE MEN WHO MADE IT, Nat Shapiro and Nat Hentoff. Louis Armstrong, Fats Waller, Jo Jones, Clarence Williams, Billy Holiday, Duke Ellington, Jelly Roll Morton and dozens of other jazz greats tell how it was in Chicago's South Side, New Orleans, depression Harlem and the modern West Coast as jazz was born and grew. xvi + 429pp.

21726-4 Paperbound $2.50

FABLES OF AESOP, translated by Sir Roger L'Estrange. A reproduction of the very rare 1931 Paris edition; a selection of the most interesting fables, together with 50 imaginative drawings by Alexander Calder. v + 128pp. 6½x9¼.

21780-9 Paperbound $1.50

AGAINST THE GRAIN (A REBOURS), Joris K. Huysmans. Filled with weird images, evidences of a bizarre imagination, exotic experiments with hallucinatory drugs, rich tastes and smells and the diversions of its sybarite hero Duc Jean des Esseintes, this classic novel pushed 19th-century literary decadence to its limits. Full unabridged edition. Do not confuse this with abridged editions generally sold. Introduction by Havelock Ellis. xlix + 206pp. 22190-3 Paperbound $2.00

VARIORUM SHAKESPEARE: HAMLET. Edited by Horace H. Furness; a landmark of American scholarship. Exhaustive footnotes and appendices treat all doubtful words and phrases, as well as suggested critical emendations throughout the play's history. First volume contains editor's own text, collated with all Quartos and Folios. Second volume contains full first Quarto, translations of Shakespeare's sources (Belleforest, and Saxo Grammaticus), Der Bestrafte Brudermord, and many essays on critical and historical points of interest by major authorities of past and present. Includes details of staging and costuming over the years. By far the best edition available for serious students of Shakespeare. Total of xx + 905pp.
21004-9, 21005-7, 2 volumes, Paperbound $7.00

A LIFE OF WILLIAM SHAKESPEARE, Sir Sidney Lee. This is the standard life of Shakespeare, summarizing everything known about Shakespeare and his plays. Incredibly rich in material, broad in coverage, clear and judicious, it has served thousands as the best introduction to Shakespeare. 1931 edition. 9 plates. xxix + 792pp. (USO) 21967-4 Paperbound $3.75

MASTERS OF THE DRAMA, John Gassner. Most comprehensive history of the drama in print, covering every tradition from Greeks to modern Europe and America, including India, Far East, etc. Covers more than 800 dramatists, 2000 plays, with biographical material, plot summaries, theatre history, criticism, etc. "Best of its kind in English," New Republic. 77 illustrations. xxii + 890pp.
20100-7 Clothbound $8.50

THE EVOLUTION OF THE ENGLISH LANGUAGE, George McKnight. The growth of English, from the 14th century to the present. Unusual, non-technical account presents basic information in very interesting form: sound shifts, change in grammar and syntax, vocabulary growth, similar topics. Abundantly illustrated with quotations. Formerly Modern English in the Making. xii + 590pp.
21932-1 Paperbound $3.50

AN ETYMOLOGICAL DICTIONARY OF MODERN ENGLISH, Ernest Weekley. Fullest, richest work of its sort, by foremost British lexicographer. Detailed word histories, including many colloquial and archaic words; extensive quotations. Do not confuse this with the Concise Etymological Dictionary, which is much abridged. Total of xxvii + 830pp. 6½ x 9¼.
21873-2, 21874-0 Two volumes, Paperbound $6.00

FLATLAND: A ROMANCE OF MANY DIMENSIONS, E. A. Abbott. Classic of science-fiction explores ramifications of life in a two-dimensional world, and what happens when a three-dimensional being intrudes. Amusing reading, but also useful as introduction to thought about hyperspace. Introduction by Banesh Hoffmann. 16 illustrations. xx + 103pp. 20001-9 Paperbound $1.00

POEMS OF ANNE BRADSTREET, edited with an introduction by Robert Hutchinson. A new selection of poems by America's first poet and perhaps the first significant woman poet in the English language. 48 poems display her development in works of considerable variety—love poems, domestic poems, religious meditations, formal elegies, "quaternions," etc. Notes, bibliography. viii + 222pp.

22160-1 Paperbound $2.50

THREE GOTHIC NOVELS: THE CASTLE OF OTRANTO BY HORACE WALPOLE; VATHEK BY WILLIAM BECKFORD; THE VAMPYRE BY JOHN POLIDORI, WITH FRAGMENT OF A NOVEL BY LORD BYRON, edited by E. F. Bleiler. The first Gothic novel, by Walpole; the finest Oriental tale in English, by Beckford; powerful Romantic supernatural story in versions by Polidori and Byron. All extremely important in history of literature; all still exciting, packed with supernatural thrills, ghosts, haunted castles, magic, etc. xl + 291pp.

21232-7 Paperbound $2.50

THE BEST TALES OF HOFFMANN, E. T. A. Hoffmann. 10 of Hoffmann's most important stories, in modern re-editings of standard translations: Nutcracker and the King of Mice, Signor Formica, Automata, The Sandman, Rath Krespel, The Golden Flowerpot, Master Martin the Cooper, The Mines of Falun, The King's Betrothed, A New Year's Eve Adventure. 7 illustrations by Hoffmann. Edited by E. F. Bleiler. xxxix + 419pp. 21793-0 Paperbound $3.00

GHOST AND HORROR STORIES OF AMBROSE BIERCE, Ambrose Bierce. 23 strikingly modern stories of the horrors latent in the human mind: The Eyes of the Panther, The Damned Thing, An Occurrence at Owl Creek Bridge, An Inhabitant of Carcosa, etc., plus the dream-essay, Visions of the Night. Edited by E. F. Bleiler. xxii + 199pp. 20767-6 Paperbound $1.50

BEST GHOST STORIES OF J. S. LEFANU, J. Sheridan LeFanu. Finest stories by Victorian master often considered greatest supernatural writer of all. Carmilla, Green Tea, The Haunted Baronet, The Familiar, and 12 others. Most never before available in the U. S. A. Edited by E. F. Bleiler. 8 illustrations from Victorian publications. xvii + 467pp. 20415-4 Paperbound $3.00

MATHEMATICAL FOUNDATIONS OF INFORMATION THEORY, A. I. Khinchin. Comprehensive introduction to work of Shannon, McMillan, Feinstein and Khinchin, placing these investigations on a rigorous mathematical basis. Covers entropy concept in probability theory, uniqueness theorem, Shannon's inequality, ergodic sources, the E property, martingale concept, noise, Feinstein's fundamental lemma, Shanon's first and second theorems. Translated by R. A. Silverman and M. D. Friedman. iii + 120pp. 60434-9 Paperbound $1.75

SEVEN SCIENCE FICTION NOVELS, H. G. Wells. The standard collection of the great novels. Complete, unabridged. *First Men in the Moon, Island of Dr. Moreau, War of the Worlds, Food of the Gods, Invisible Man, Time Machine, In the Days of the Comet.* Not only science fiction fans, but every educated person owes it to himself to read these novels. 1015pp. (USO) 20264-X Clothbound $5.00

LAST AND FIRST MEN AND STAR MAKER, TWO SCIENCE FICTION NOVELS, Olaf Stapledon. Greatest future histories in science fiction. In the first, human intelligence is the "hero," through strange paths of evolution, interplanetary invasions, incredible technologies, near extinctions and reemergences. Star Maker describes the quest of a band of star rovers for intelligence itself, through time and space: weird inhuman civilizations, crustacean minds, symbiotic worlds, etc. Complete, unabridged. v + 438pp. (USO) 21962-3 Paperbound $2.50

THREE PROPHETIC NOVELS, H. G. WELLS. Stages of a consistently planned future for mankind. *When the Sleeper Wakes,* and *A Story of the Days to Come,* anticipate *Brave New World* and *1984,* in the 21st Century; *The Time Machine,* only complete version in print, shows farther future and the end of mankind. All show Wells's greatest gifts as storyteller and novelist. Edited by E. F. Bleiler. x + 335pp. (USO) 20605-X Paperbound $2.50

THE DEVIL'S DICTIONARY, Ambrose Bierce. America's own Oscar Wilde—Ambrose Bierce—offers his barbed iconoclastic wisdom in over 1,000 definitions hailed by H. L. Mencken as "some of the most gorgeous witticisms in the English language." 145pp. 20487-1 Paperbound $1.25

MAX AND MORITZ, Wilhelm Busch. Great children's classic, father of comic strip, of two bad boys, Max and Moritz. Also Ker and Plunk (Plisch und Plumm), Cat and Mouse, Deceitful Henry, Ice-Peter, The Boy and the Pipe, and five other pieces. Original German, with English translation. Edited by H. Arthur Klein; translations by various hands and H. Arthur Klein. vi + 216pp.
20181-3 Paperbound $2.00

PIGS IS PIGS AND OTHER FAVORITES, Ellis Parker Butler. The title story is one of the best humor short stories, as Mike Flannery obfuscates biology and English. Also included, That Pup of Murchison's, The Great American Pie Company, and Perkins of Portland. 14 illustrations. v + 109pp. 21532-6 Paperbound $1.25

THE PETERKIN PAPERS, Lucretia P. Hale. It takes genius to be as stupidly mad as the Peterkins, as they decide to become wise, celebrate the "Fourth," keep a cow, and otherwise strain the resources of the Lady from Philadelphia. Basic book of American humor. 153 illustrations. 219pp. 20794-3 Paperbound $1.50

PERRAULT'S FAIRY TALES, translated by A. E. Johnson and S. R. Littlewood, with 34 full-page illustrations by Gustave Doré. All the original Perrault stories—Cinderella, Sleeping Beauty, Bluebeard, Little Red Riding Hood, Puss in Boots, Tom Thumb, etc.—with their witty verse morals and the magnificent illustrations of Doré. One of the five or six great books of European fairy tales. viii + 117pp. 8⅛ x 11. 22311-6 Paperbound $2.00

OLD HUNGARIAN FAIRY TALES, Baroness Orczy. Favorites translated and adapted by author of the *Scarlet Pimpernel.* Eight fairy tales include "The Suitors of Princess Fire-Fly," "The Twin Hunchbacks," "Mr. Cuttlefish's Love Story," and "The Enchanted Cat." This little volume of magic and adventure will captivate children as it has for generations. 90 drawings by Montagu Barstow. 96pp.
22293-4 Paperbound $1.95

THE RED FAIRY BOOK, Andrew Lang. Lang's color fairy books have long been children's favorites. This volume includes Rapunzel, Jack and the Bean-stalk and 35 other stories, familiar and unfamiliar. 4 plates, 93 illustrations x + 367pp.
21673-X Paperbound $2.50

THE BLUE FAIRY BOOK, Andrew Lang. Lang's tales come from all countries and all times. Here are 37 tales from Grimm, the Arabian Nights, Greek Mythology, and other fascinating sources. 8 plates, 130 illustrations. xi + 390pp.
21437-0 Paperbound $2.50

HOUSEHOLD STORIES BY THE BROTHERS GRIMM. Classic English-language edition of the well-known tales — Rumpelstiltskin, Snow White, Hansel and Gretel, The Twelve Brothers, Faithful John, Rapunzel, Tom Thumb (52 stories in all). Translated into simple, straightforward English by Lucy Crane. Ornamented with headpieces, vignettes, elaborate decorative initials and a dozen full-page illustrations by Walter Crane. x + 269pp.
21080-4 Paperbound $2.00

THE MERRY ADVENTURES OF ROBIN HOOD, Howard Pyle. The finest modern versions of the traditional ballads and tales about the great English outlaw. Howard Pyle's complete prose version, with every word, every illustration of the first edition. Do not confuse this facsimile of the original (1883) with modern editions that change text or illustrations. 23 plates plus many page decorations. xxii + 296pp.
22043-5 Paperbound $2.50

THE STORY OF KING ARTHUR AND HIS KNIGHTS, Howard Pyle. The finest children's version of the life of King Arthur; brilliantly retold by Pyle, with 48 of his most imaginative illustrations. xviii + 313pp. 6⅛ x 9¼.
21445-1 Paperbound $2.50

THE WONDERFUL WIZARD OF OZ, L. Frank Baum. America's finest children's book in facsimile of first edition with all Denslow illustrations in full color. The edition a child should have. Introduction by Martin Gardner. 23 color plates, scores of drawings. iv + 267pp.
20691-2 Paperbound $2.50

THE MARVELOUS LAND OF OZ, L. Frank Baum. The second Oz book, every bit as imaginative as the Wizard. The hero is a boy named Tip, but the Scarecrow and the Tin Woodman are back, as is the Oz magic. 16 color plates, 120 drawings by John R. Neill. 287pp.
20692-0 Paperbound $2.50

THE MAGICAL MONARCH OF MO, L. Frank Baum. Remarkable adventures in a land even stranger than Oz. The best of Baum's books not in the Oz series. 15 color plates and dozens of drawings by Frank Verbeck. xviii + 237pp.
21892-9 Paperbound $2.25

THE BAD CHILD'S BOOK OF BEASTS, MORE BEASTS FOR WORSE CHILDREN, A MORAL ALPHABET, Hilaire Belloc. Three complete humor classics in one volume. Be kind to the frog, and do not call him names . . . and 28 other whimsical animals. Familiar favorites and some not so well known. Illustrated by Basil Blackwell. 156pp.
(USO) 20749-8 Paperbound $1.50

EAST O' THE SUN AND WEST O' THE MOON, George W. Dasent. Considered the best of all translations of these Norwegian folk tales, this collection has been enjoyed by generations of children (and folklorists too). Includes True and Untrue, Why the Sea is Salt, East O' the Sun and West O' the Moon, Why the Bear is Stumpy-Tailed, Boots and the Troll, The Cock and the Hen, Rich Peter the Pedlar, and 52 more. The only edition with all 59 tales. 77 illustrations by Erik Werenskiold and Theodor Kittelsen. xv + 418pp. 22521-6 Paperbound $3.50

GOOPS AND HOW TO BE THEM, Gelett Burgess. Classic of tongue-in-cheek humor, masquerading as etiquette book. 87 verses, twice as many cartoons, show mischievous Goops as they demonstrate to children virtues of table manners, neatness, courtesy, etc. Favorite for generations. viii + 88pp. 6½ x 9¼.
22233-0 Paperbound $1.25

ALICE'S ADVENTURES UNDER GROUND, Lewis Carroll. The first version, quite different from the final *Alice in Wonderland,* printed out by Carroll himself with his own illustrations. Complete facsimile of the "million dollar" manuscript Carroll gave to Alice Liddell in 1864. Introduction by Martin Gardner. viii + 96pp. Title and dedication pages in color. 21482-6 Paperbound $1.25

THE BROWNIES, THEIR BOOK, Palmer Cox. Small as mice, cunning as foxes, exuberant and full of mischief, the Brownies go to the zoo, toy shop, seashore, circus, etc., in 24 verse adventures and 266 illustrations. Long a favorite, since their first appearance in St. Nicholas Magazine. xi + 144pp. 6⅝ x 9¼.
21265-3 Paperbound $1.75

SONGS OF CHILDHOOD, Walter De La Mare. Published (under the pseudonym Walter Ramal) when De La Mare was only 29, this charming collection has long been a favorite children's book. A facsimile of the first edition in paper, the 47 poems capture the simplicity of the nursery rhyme and the ballad, including such lyrics as I Met Eve, Tartary, The Silver Penny. vii + 106pp. (USO) 21972-0 Paperbound $1.25

THE COMPLETE NONSENSE OF EDWARD LEAR, Edward Lear. The finest 19th-century humorist-cartoonist in full: all nonsense limericks, zany alphabets, Owl and Pussycat, songs, nonsense botany, and more than 500 illustrations by Lear himself. Edited by Holbrook Jackson. xxix + 287pp. (USO) 20167-8 Paperbound $2.00

BILLY WHISKERS: THE AUTOBIOGRAPHY OF A GOAT, Frances Trego Montgomery. A favorite of children since the early 20th century, here are the escapades of that rambunctious, irresistible and mischievous goat—Billy Whiskers. Much in the spirit of *Peck's Bad Boy,* this is a book that children never tire of reading or hearing. All the original familiar illustrations by W. H. Fry are included: 6 color plates, 18 black and white drawings. 159pp. 22345-0 Paperbound $2.00

MOTHER GOOSE MELODIES. Faithful republication of the fabulously rare Munroe and Francis "copyright 1833" Boston edition—the most important Mother Goose collection, usually referred to as the "original." Familiar rhymes plus many rare ones, with wonderful old woodcut illustrations. Edited by E. F. Bleiler. 128pp. 4½ x 6⅜. 22577-1 Paperbound $1.00

TWO LITTLE SAVAGES; BEING THE ADVENTURES OF TWO BOYS WHO LIVED AS INDIANS AND WHAT THEY LEARNED, Ernest Thompson Seton. Great classic of nature and boyhood provides a vast range of woodlore in most palatable form, a genuinely entertaining story. Two farm boys build a teepee in woods and live in it for a month, working out Indian solutions to living problems, star lore, birds and animals, plants, etc. 293 illustrations. vii + 286pp.

20985-7 Paperbound $2.50

PETER PIPER'S PRACTICAL PRINCIPLES OF PLAIN & PERFECT PRONUNCIATION. Alliterative jingles and tongue-twisters of surprising charm, that made their first appearance in America about 1830. Republished in full with the spirited woodcut illustrations from this earliest American edition. 32pp. $4\frac{1}{2}$ x $6\frac{3}{8}$.

22560-7 Paperbound $1.00

SCIENCE EXPERIMENTS AND AMUSEMENTS FOR CHILDREN, Charles Vivian. 73 easy experiments, requiring only materials found at home or easily available, such as candles, coins, steel wool, etc.; illustrate basic phenomena like vacuum, simple chemical reaction, etc. All safe. Modern, well-planned. Formerly *Science Games for Children*. 102 photos, numerous drawings. 96pp. $6\frac{1}{8}$ x $9\frac{1}{4}$.

21856-2 Paperbound $1.25

AN INTRODUCTION TO CHESS MOVES AND TACTICS SIMPLY EXPLAINED, Leonard Barden. Informal intermediate introduction, quite strong in explaining reasons for moves. Covers basic material, tactics, important openings, traps, positional play in middle game, end game. Attempts to isolate patterns and recurrent configurations. Formerly *Chess*. 58 figures. 102pp.   (USO) 21210-6 Paperbound $1.25

LASKER'S MANUAL OF CHESS, Dr. Emanuel Lasker. Lasker was not only one of the five great World Champions, he was also one of the ablest expositors, theorists, and analysts. In many ways, his Manual, permeated with his philosophy of battle, filled with keen insights, is one of the greatest works ever written on chess. Filled with analyzed games by the great players. A single-volume library that will profit almost any chess player, beginner or master. 308 diagrams. xli x 349pp.

20640-8 Paperbound $2.75

THE MASTER BOOK OF MATHEMATICAL RECREATIONS, Fred Schuh. In opinion of many the finest work ever prepared on mathematical puzzles, stunts, recreations; exhaustively thorough explanations of mathematics involved, analysis of effects, citation of puzzles and games. Mathematics involved is elementary. Translated by F. Göbel. 194 figures. xxiv + 430pp.   22134-2 Paperbound $3.00

MATHEMATICS, MAGIC AND MYSTERY, Martin Gardner. Puzzle editor for Scientific American explains mathematics behind various mystifying tricks: card tricks, stage "mind reading," coin and match tricks, counting out games, geometric dissections, etc. Probability sets, theory of numbers clearly explained. Also provides more than 400 tricks, guaranteed to work, that you can do. 135 illustrations. xii + 176pp.

20335-2 Paperbound $1.50

MATHEMATICAL PUZZLES FOR BEGINNERS AND ENTHUSIASTS, Geoffrey Mott-Smith. 189 puzzles from easy to difficult—involving arithmetic, logic, algebra, properties of digits, probability, etc.—for enjoyment and mental stimulus. Explanation of mathematical principles behind the puzzles. 135 illustrations. viii + 248pp.
20198-8 Paperbound $1.75

PAPER FOLDING FOR BEGINNERS, William D. Murray and Francis J. Rigney. Easiest book on the market, clearest instructions on making interesting, beautiful origami. Sail boats, cups, roosters, frogs that move legs, bonbon boxes, standing birds, etc. 40 projects; more than 275 diagrams and photographs. 94pp.
20713-7 Paperbound $1.00

TRICKS AND GAMES ON THE POOL TABLE, Fred Herrmann. 79 tricks and games—some solitaires, some for two or more players, some competitive games—to entertain you between formal games. Mystifying shots and throws, unusual caroms, tricks involving such props as cork, coins, a hat, etc. Formerly *Fun on the Pool Table*. 77 figures. 95pp.
21814-7 Paperbound $1.00

HAND SHADOWS TO BE THROWN UPON THE WALL: A SERIES OF NOVEL AND AMUSING FIGURES FORMED BY THE HAND, Henry Bursill. Delightful picturebook from great-grandfather's day shows how to make 18 different hand shadows: a bird that flies, duck that quacks, dog that wags his tail, camel, goose, deer, boy, turtle, etc. Only book of its sort. vi + 33pp. 6½ x 9¼. 21779-5 Paperbound $1.00

WHITTLING AND WOODCARVING, E. J. Tangerman. 18th printing of best book on market. "If you can cut a potato you can carve" toys and puzzles, chains, chessmen, caricatures, masks, frames, woodcut blocks, surface patterns, much more. Information on tools, woods, techniques. Also goes into serious wood sculpture from Middle Ages to present, East and West. 464 photos, figures. x + 293pp.
20965-2 Paperbound $2.00

HISTORY OF PHILOSOPHY, Julián Marías. Possibly the clearest, most easily followed, best planned, most useful one-volume history of philosophy on the market; neither skimpy nor overfull. Full details on system of every major philosopher and dozens of less important thinkers from pre-Socratics up to Existentialism and later. Strong on many European figures usually omitted. Has gone through dozens of editions in Europe. 1966 edition, translated by Stanley Appelbaum and Clarence Strowbridge. xviii + 505pp. 21739-6 Paperbound $3.50

YOGA: A SCIENTIFIC EVALUATION, Kovoor T. Behanan. Scientific but non-technical study of physiological results of yoga exercises; done under auspices of Yale U. Relations to Indian thought, to psychoanalysis, etc. 16 photos. xxiii + 270pp.
20505-3 Paperbound $2.50

Prices subject to change without notice.
Available at your book dealer or write for free catalogue to Dept. GI, Dover Publications, Inc., 180 Varick St., N. Y., N. Y. 10014. Dover publishes more than 150 books each year on science, elementary and advanced mathematics, biology, music, art, literary history, social sciences and other areas.